Archaeology and the
Pan-European Romanesque

DUCKWORTH DEBATES IN ARCHAEOLOGY

Series editor: Richard Hodges

Against Cultural Property John Carman
Archaeology: The Conceptual Challenge Timothy Insoll
Archaeology and Text John Moreland
Archaeology and the Pan-European Romanesque Tadhg O'Keeffe
Beyond Celts, Germans and Scythians Peter Wells
Combat Archaeology John Schofield
Debating the Archaeological Heritage Robin Skeates
Early Islamic Syria Alan Walmsley
Gerasa and the Decapolis David Kennedy
Loot, Legitimacy and Ownership Colin Renfrew
The Origins of the English Catherine Hills
Rethinking Wetland Archaeology Robert Van de Noort & Aidan O'Sullivan
The Roman Countryside Stephen Dyson
Shipwreck Archaeology of the Holy Land Sean Kingsley
Social Evolution Mark Pluciennik
State Formation in Early China Li Liu & Xingcan Chen
Towns and Trade in the Age of Charlemagne Richard Hodges
Villa to Village Riccardo Francovich and Richard Hodges

DUCKWORTH DEBATES IN ARCHAEOLOGY

Archaeology and the Pan-European Romanesque

Tadhg O'Keeffe

Duckworth

First published in 2007 by
Gerald Duckworth & Co. Ltd.
90-93 Cowcross Street, London EC1M 6BF
Tel: 020 7490 7300
Fax: 020 7490 0080
inquiries@duckworth-publishers.co.uk
www.ducknet.co.uk

A catalogue record for this book is available from the British Library

ISBN 978 07156 3434 9

Typeset by Ray Davies
Printed and bound in Great Britain by
MPG Books Limited, Bodmin, Cornwall

Contents

List of illustrations 6

Preface and acknowledgements 7

1. A critical historiography of 'the story' 13
2. Opening the Black Box 45
3. Modelling regionalism: technology and society 73
4. Discourse and translation: domains of meaning 97
5. Archaeology and Romanesque 107

Bibliography 115

Index 124

List of illustrations

Fig. 1. The monastic plan of Cluny in 1157 18
Fig. 2. San Miniato façade; St Nicolas, Civray 21
Fig. 3. Old St Peter's, Rome; Fulda; Bamberg Cathedral 22
Fig. 4. Relationships of Roman to Romance to Romanesque 32
Fig. 5. Capital from the façade of Notre-Dame-le-Grande in Poitiers 39
Fig. 6. Network of linkages in Germany, with the Netherlands and Flanders 61
Fig. 7. Broken pilaster from Hedingham Castle's great tower showing the wall's rubble core and a disfiguring down-pipe 79
Fig. 8. Two maps of Romanesque Europe: (a) the perspective that yields a single style and suggests a common vision; (b) the perspective that suggests a multiplicity of styles 94-5
Fig. 9. The nave of Tewkesbury abbey church 109

Preface and acknowledgements

The literature on the so-called Romanesque style is almost as bewilderingly large as its constituent corpus of buildings and *objets d'art*. Most parts of modern Europe have a heritage identified as Romanesque, so there is probably no local or regional journal of archaeology or history across the Continent in which the term has not made an appearance. Studies of hundreds of important artefacts and monuments, from small ivories to large cathedrals, have been published as monographs or have appeared in refereed periodicals of international circulation. Scholarly syntheses of Romanesque as an international phenomenon have been published in every major European language, with authoritative pan-European surveys of the architecture being particularly numerous. So, almost two hundred years on from the very first publications in which the term was used to describe a body of high medieval art and architecture, one could confidently claim that Romanesque is now a well known and well understood style.

This book, which is specifically about architecture, is not intended to be yet another introduction. Rather, it is directed principally at readers who already have some familiarity with the architecture and its literature, and who can therefore contextualise my critique of the interpretative scaffolding that scholarship has erected around the buildings in question. Readers will note that relatively few buildings are name-checked here: this book is mainly about Romanesque rather than about the many buildings that have been gathered under its umbrella. The distinction is an important one.

My aims in this book are threefold. The first is to articulate at length the problems that are inherent in the Romanesque construct, at least as manifest in that literature. The second is to suggest an alternative conceptualisation of the large-scale trajectories of architectural change during a critical period in European history. The third is to begin a process of reclaiming as a topic of archaeological enquiry the collected material that is taken to constitute 'the Romanesque'. If the book has an over-arching aim it is this: to wrest the reins of interpretation of eleventh- and twelfth-century architecture from the *exclusive* grip of the chevron-hunters and corbel-table-chronologists who would have us believe that the adjective 'Romanesque' is explanatory.

The key word in the title of this series, *Debates*, has licensed me to pursue this agenda through a text that is opinionated and argumentative, as well as to articulate my opposition to the dominance of a particular tradition of scholarship, especially within the field of Art History, that has developed with respect to this architecture. My text deliberately eschews the balance and even-handedness (though not, I hope, the honesty) that would be required in a text-book. Instead, it argues a point of view. Although he might reject having his book characterised in such terms, John Moreland's *Archaeology and Text*, also published in this series, was an exemplar of sorts. To debate is to take sides, to match conviction with courage, and to interchange between rhetoric and argument. I hope that my book is read in that spirit.

The series title has also allowed me to write 'archaeologically' for a readership of archaeologists weaned on the writings of people like Michael Shanks and Christopher Tilley. Let me elaborate on this point. I confess that I found the writing of this book, short as it is, quite difficult. The more I have reflected on

Romanesque as a category the more suspicious I have become of its underlying historical agenda and overriding contemporary value. The more conscious I have become of swimming against an intellectual tide, the more I have understood how politics in the broadest sense exert the strongest gravitational pull on that tide. Having decided that I wanted to articulate my thoughts about Romanesque *as a category*, I struggled to find a voice that would speak simultaneously to readers from two selected disciplines: Archaeology, to which I belong professionally, and Art History, in which I am also qualified and in which Romanesque traditionally belongs as a subject of study. Cross-disciplinary projects are always laudable, but it seems from my vantage point that when these two disciplines converge on medieval topics they reveal different cultures of scholarly discourse, different output-expectations of their practitioners, and, I think, different tolerance levels with respect to theoretical adventure. I decided eventually to write this book as a book about Archaeology, which I (like many other theoretically-informed archaeologists today) define not only as a technique for retrieving data, which is how historians and art historians usually understand it, but as a system of thought and discourse about the world of the present as well as of the past.

The decision to address my thoughts to one audience in particular was based on the following realisation: if the construct of Romanesque has only ever existed in the culture of scholarship, as I argue here is the case, then the only way to deal with it is through the portal of epistemology, and the only such portal that one can pass through confidently is the portal of one's own discipline.

*

The book opens with a very brief and general survey of architecture covering the period from the ninth to the mid-twelfth century, followed by a historiography (Chapter 1). In the chapters that follow I proceed to assert, and where possible to argue, three interconnected points – or at least attempt to articulate three viewpoints – about Romanesque.

In brief, the first is that the construct of the Romanesque style is an inherently unstable one. It has retained its illusion of cohesion, and so concealed its fundamentally fictive nature, by virtue of having been consigned by nineteenth- and early twentieth-century scholars to the Black Box, a metaphoric space in which is locked every concept or innovation that is regarded as no longer in need of review (Chapter 2).

The second is that the diverse architectures of eleventh- and twelfth-century Europe are not local or regional manifestations of some common, pan-Continental, ideal, as is stated or implied to be the case in virtually all of the literature, but that they represent different, heterogeneous stabilisations of an architectural inheritance that had fragmented from late Antiquity. I am not sure that Romanesque as a stylistic construct can have much value in the interrogation of individual buildings, but I concede its shorthand value at a level of synthesis – only, however, if we use it to represent collective diversity, an absence of unity that is the outcome of centrifugal forces of architectural change originating in Antiquity rather than of centripetal forces originating in the re-birthing environment of the eleventh century. I make this assertion by specific reference to the so-called 'regional schools' and their technologies (Chapter 3).

The third point is that we can only understand the meaning of the architectures traditionally described as Romanesque by downscaling our enquiry from the pan-European level (familiar to us from the syntheses of people like Kenneth Conant and Hans Erich Kubach) to the local, and by shifting from generalisation to specificity. The buildings of the eleventh and twelfth centuries were complex discursive objects of visual culture, located in, and so contributing principally to, quite localised networks of understanding (Chapter 4).

The book concludes with a revisit to that relationship between disciplines on which I have commented here. When the architecture in question first came into scholarly focus in the 1800s, its study was regarded as belonging within the discipline of Archaeology as it was then understood. By the early 1900s it had moved under the umbrella of Art History (or, more precisely, the boundaries between Archaeology and Art History shifted, leaving Romanesque located within the latter). I argue that the content of Romanesque needs reinvestment by the discipline of Archaeology as we – archaeologists – know it today, precisely because there is reluctance among art historians to subject the architecture to the type of critique that they allow with respect to more contemporary buildings (Chapter 5).

*

My thanks to Richard Hodges for accepting this book into the *Debates in Archaeology* series. As it spent rather longer in gestation than I had anticipated – its progress was delayed by the arrival of the little girl to whom it is now dedicated! – I owe Deborah Blake at Duckworth an enormous debt for her exceptional patience. A President's Research Fellowship from University College Dublin afforded me the time away from teaching and administration to read widely and to think about some of the issues in this book, and I am pleased to acknowledge here the generosity of the award. Margaret and Evan both played a part in the life-story of this book, and to them my thanks and love, as always.

For little Anneliese

1

A critical historiography of 'the story'

Introduction: a renaissance building boom

Despite a relatively slow start between the fifth and eighth centuries, large parts of Europe experienced building booms right through the medieval period. The closing centuries of the first millennium saw the beginning of an extraordinary phase of church and castle construction in both rural and urban environments, the staggering momentum of which did not let up for any significant duration across most of that vast geographical space until the fourteenth century. Judging by the surviving architectural record, the peak period of building activity right across the Continent was probably between the middle of the eleventh century and the end of the thirteenth. Those buildings constructed in the century and a half between about 1000 and 1150 are the ones of particular concern to us in this book. I will begin this chapter by presenting a very general overview of their framing architectural history, before turning to review its historiography.

The majority of the eleventh- and twelfth-century ecclesiastical and élite-secular buildings in question are regarded as constituting a coherent group, and have been so regarded since the early 1800s. This is largely because certain design features, many of them ostensibly of Roman origin, are identified as common to them. It is also because of historical context. The period between the mid-eleventh and mid-twelfth centuries in particular is identified as a period of renaissance: although the dates do not fit a designated calendrical century, this is the so-called 'renaissance of the twelfth century' (Haskins 1927; Benson and Constable 1982; Swanson 1999). The buildings, particularly the ecclesiastical ones, are understood to be products of, and in some instances actual deliberate manifestations of, a re-birthing ideology.

The dates of 1000-1150 that I have selected for this book are, of course, arbitrary. Why have I selected them? Taking the last date first, by 1150 a new architectural 'movement' – we know it as Gothic – was under way. Its birthplace is identified as the Ile de France, hitherto a region of strikingly low-key architectural endeavour. The east end of the French royal abbey church of St Denis, located outside Paris, had been rebuilt in the late 1120s and early 1130s using a new technology and a new design, and in the second half of the twelfth century these new structural and aesthetic principles began their trans-Continental diffusion. Gothic forms were not truly universal in Europe until the middle of the thirteenth century, but the implications of the new work at St Denis and elsewhere in the Paris Basin were being absorbed to some degree in major new building projects after 1150 (for general context see Bony 1983). Hence that date.

The earlier date of 1000 is less arbitrary. On the whole, scholars who treat the architecture of the 'twelfth-century renaissance' as constituting a single stylistic movement tend to prefer the date of 1050, but 1000 has the advantage of being the millennium year and therefore of marking a (contemporaneously and retrospectively) recognised chronological watershed (Focillon 1953). There is evidence that people across Europe feared that the change from one millennium to the next would bring with it the fate that had been promised for the world in the Book of Revelation (Landes 2000). Once that year passed without incident, there was, according to the unequivocal, contemporary testimony of Rodulfus Glaber, a great explosion of new churches:

> Just before the third year after the millennium, throughout the whole world, but most especially in Italy and Gaul, men began to reconstruct churches, although for the most part the existing ones were properly built and not in the least unworthy. But it seemed as though each Christian community [was] aiming to surpass all others in splendour of construction. It was as if the whole world were shaking itself free, shrugging off the burden of the past, and cladding itself everywhere in a white mantle of churches. Almost all the episcopal churches and those of monasteries dedicated to various saints, and little village chapels, were rebuilt better than before by the faithful (Hiscock 2003: xix).

The surviving architectural record generally supports this claim, although there are two caveats. First, it is clear in retrospect that the 'white mantle of churches' was not quite the overnight phenomenon that Glaber claimed it to be. It is apparent now that the increase should really be seen in the context of an upward trajectory of building activity from the 800s and 900s rather than as a very dramatic trend-reversal linked to millennialism (Plant 2003); it is also apparent, in fact, that ecclesiastical reform movements during the 1000s probably generated greater surges of localised building activity than the simple deliverance from potential apocalypse in January 1001 had done. Second, Glaber's identification of Italy and Gaul as the places where the immediate post-1000 'white mantle of churches' was most in evidence simply reflects his experience of a small part of Europe rather than his knowledge of the entire Continent, and is hard to assess quantitatively even today.

Notwithstanding these caveats, the corpus of known (and

known to have existed) post-1000 buildings is sufficiently large when measured against the pre-1000 corpus for us to choose *l'an mil*, the millennium year, as our other boundary date.

A period church: Cluny III

The sheer number and diversity of church buildings erected in the eleventh and early twelfth centuries makes generalisation about their architecture very difficult, but the bigger churches of the period do have a sufficient range of recurring features for us to compile a check-list of sorts.

Ground plans tend to follow traditional early Christian norms in having three aisles or, less commonly, five. There is usually a transept at the east end of the nave, and sometimes also at the west end. The east end may have an apse enclosed within the end wall, but the more common format is a projecting apse flanked by two or four projecting apsidal chapels, all served by an ambulatory. Chapels, square-ended or apsidal, also project from the east walls of the transepts. Towers may ascend as projecting structures at the west or may rise above the crossing. Internal elevations are bay-divided through the provision of vertical wall-ribs at regular intervals; these ribs may carry the supporting arches of vaults or they may simply stop at the wall-head. Internal elevations are usually two- or three-storeyed; the lower storeys are comprised almost entirely of arches and their supports, but the upper storeys have flush wall surfaces perforated by windows or gallery openings, or both. Wall surfaces, internal and external, are an important ingredient in the architecture: the visitor senses that the main liturgical spaces are defined by walls, however perforated by arches and embellished by arcading they may be, whereas in a great church of the thirteenth century the walls will often seem to have been replaced by narrow supports, giving the whole structure a transparent gauze-like quality. Externally, there is an affect of 'massing' in the eleventh- and earlier twelfth-century architecture, particularly at the east end of churches: the different sizes and shapes of the component parts of the architecture will be presented in the elevations and vistas of a building in such a way that an observer's eye will often be carried inwards and upwards from large structural block to small structural block. The churches are generally vaulted, with barrels, groins or ribs, but this is not a diagnostic feature of the architecture: some of the greatest churches (Ely and Peterborough in England, for example) were timber-roofed. The round arch is a recurring feature, although it is present in all the earlier architectural traditions as well. Pointed arches were used in this architecture, but mainly only for the transverse arches of vaults.

To give a more tangible impression of the type of architecture being erected during this period, as well as of its historical context, let me turn very briefly to one of the greatest buildings of the era, Cluny in Burgundy (Conant 1959; 1968; Armi 1983). More than any other building, this encompasses fully the nature of the period we are reviewing, even if we must stop short of describing it as 'typical'.

Cluny was a monastery founded in 910. Its community followed the Rule of St Benedict (*c.* 480-543), as did many contemporary monastic communities across Europe. During the tenth century its brethren adapted the Rule to their own needs, enriching especially its liturgical dimension. The outcome was that the monastery became the centre of, and also the eponym for, an autonomous Benedictine monastic movement: the Cluniac.

The history of building activity at the parent site is an unambiguous indicator of increasing community size and increasing wealth between its early tenth-century foundation and 1130, the completion-date of its last great building project. The original early tenth-century church, known as Cluny I, was insufficient for the growing community and was replaced by a new church, Cluny II, erected over a period of a quarter of a century, starting in 955. Its replacement, Cluny III, built over a period of more than four decades (1088-1130) to accommodate a community of many hundreds, was to the north of Cluny II, presumably to allow the latter remain in use until the larger new version was completed; Cluny II was eventually swallowed up in the claustral courts of Cluny III (Fig. 1).

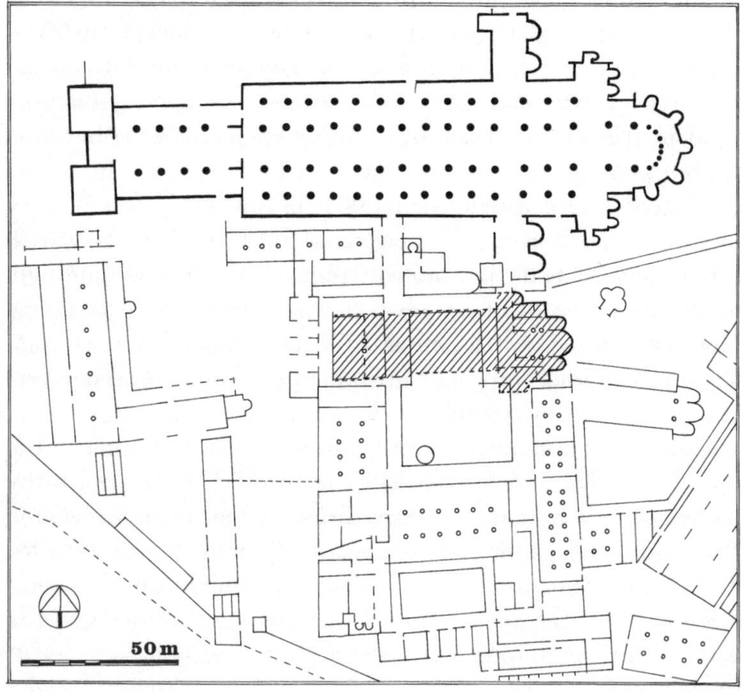

Fig. 1. The monastic plan of Cluny in 1157, showing the great phase III church to the north and the remains of the earlier, phase II, church to its south (after Conant)

The church of Cluny III had a monumentality appropriate to the community's sense of pre-eminence among Europe's Benedictine congregations. Now almost entirely lost to us, thanks to the zeal for demolition of French revolutionaries between 1800 and 1810, we know of its extraordinary character both from early descriptions and illustrations, and from Kenneth Conant's excavation at the site. We also know a little of the experience of being inside it, because a number of its smaller stylistic descendents – Autun, Beaune, La-Charité-sur-Loire and, especially, Paray-le-Monial – still survive. We also know about Cluny III's church from its precursor, St Philibert at Tournus: although Cluny III seems to have differed from Tournus in having pointed arches, an assortment of Classical features, and 'peeled-back' wall surfaces, its tall arcades, its narrow, non-galleried triforium with a single light per bay, and its triple-light-per-bay clerestory are features that had been used earlier at Tournus (Armi 2004: 174-5).

Cluny III's church had a long, five-bay, western narthex with a twin-tower façade, beyond which the church proper had twin aisles on each side of its nave. It was fully sixteen bays long from east to west, with two pairs of transepts at the east end. The interior was vaulted: the main spaces had pointed barrel vaults – made by adopting brick-building technology (Armi 2004: 85)? – supported by transverse arches that marked the bay divisions. Those arches were supported externally by early examples of flying buttresses; it has been suggested that these were added after a vault collapse in 1125 (Stalley 1999: 139). The church's massing, the towers, and the semicircular ambulatory with its chapels are all features of the new architecture of the era, even if the vaulting was somewhat precocious in being pointed. Inside, arch capitals and other important structural members carried sculptural decoration, and the few surviving fragments testify to the quality of the workmanship.

Genealogy

When new church buildings were required in the early part of the eleventh century, it was the Roman building tradition of many centuries earlier that provided the exemplars. Cluny III's church, for example, was clearly designed with an eye on the original St Peter's in Rome: St Peter was one of its dedicatees (St Paul was the other), and a range of its features – fluted pilasters, Corinthianesque capitals, egg-and-dart-like ornament, a lack of galleries – expressly referenced Roman architecture.

While Cluny III and buildings like it provide the most dramatic evidence of the presence of Roman ideas in high medieval culture, it should be noted that the intelligentsia of eleventh-century Europe quarried the Roman past for all sorts of other motifs, literary, political and rhetorical. In fact, the renaissance identified by scholars as beginning around the mid-point of that century is regarded specifically as a renaissance of *romanitas*, of Latinity. As Erwin Panofsky expressed it, the Roman past represented in the twelfth century a world that demanded to be approached not historically but pragmatically. It was 'something far off yet, in a sense, still alive and, therefore, at once potentially useful and potentially dangerous' (Panofsky 1960: 110-11).

Roman architectural exemplars were actually accessible directly in relatively few parts of eleventh-century Europe. The northern Italian cities of Rome, Ravenna and Milan had the greatest number of extant and still-used churches from the end of the Roman period (McClendon 2005: 3-22), so it is hardly surprising that new buildings of the region in the 1000s and 1100s – San Miniato, for example (Fig. 2 *left*) – are so explicitly in debt to the older monuments that the casual visitor could easily confuse them for works of the earlier period. Roman architecture was more fragmentary elsewhere within the old imperial boundaries, especially in trans-Alpine locales, but even those fragments constituted a tangible medium through which the ancient civilisation could be revisited (see Rebourg 1993 for Autun, for instance). It is no co-incidence, for example, that façades in western French churches of the 1100s (see Seidel 1981) often reveal their origin in the architecture of the Roman triumphal arches of Gaul, as in the example of Civray (Fig. 2 *right*).

Fig. 2. *left*: San Miniato façade; *right*: St Nicolas, Civray.

On the whole, access to Roman work was so limited outside the Mediterranean lands that the closest encounters many eleventh- and twelfth-century builders in northern Europe had with the built fabric of *romanitas* was actually through its mediated form in the so-called renaissances of the Carolingians (McKitterick 1994) and Ottonians (Reuter 1991). The new churches that were erected during those two sequential renaissances were Roman-like in many respects, and often had Roman *spolia*, but they were fundamentally different from their Roman models as well as from each other. Those differences are many and have been documented by other writers (see Heitz 1980 and Grodecki 1958) for the Carolingians and Ottonians respectively). Exemplifying the relationship, Old St Peter's in Rome (built 320-30), for example, which had a western transept, was clearly the inspiration for Fulda, a

Carolingian church of *c.* 802 which had a western transept, and yet Fulda was no imitation of it (McClendon 2005: 5-6; 158-61). Fulda, in turn, inspired a number of Ottonian buildings with single western transepts, such as the cathedral of Bamberg, consecrated in 1012 (von Winterfeld 1979), but, again, it was not actually imitated in those later works (Fig. 3).

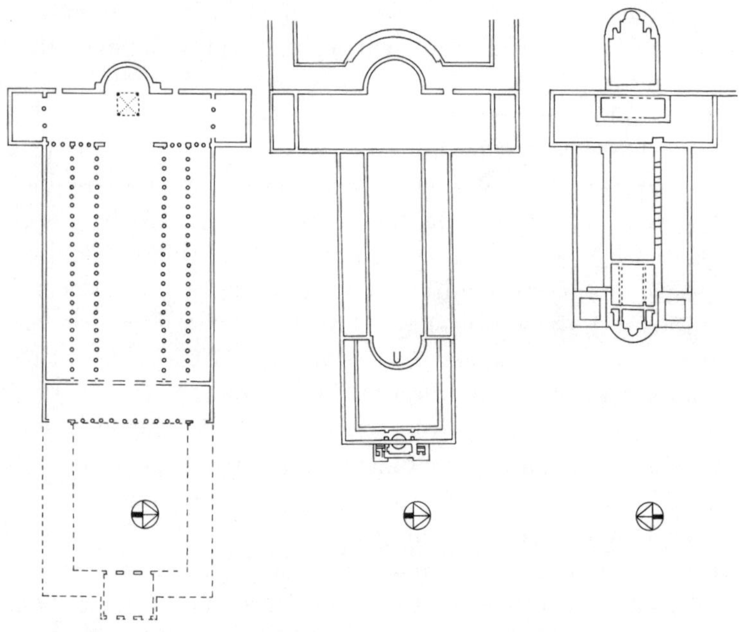

Fig. 3. *left*: Old St Peter's, Rome; *centre*: Fulda; *right*: Bamberg Cathedral.

While the so-called renaissance of the twelfth century is identified with Roman cultural revivalism, it would clearly be quite wrong to imagine that the long period between the start of the fifth century (when the Roman world was transformed by 'barbarian' incursions) and the middle of the eleventh had no active and continuous culture of *romanitas*. On the contrary, there was virtually no aspect of cultural practice among Europeans of the second half of the first millennium AD that did not owe an on-going debt to pre-400 Roman culture (see McCormick 2002, for example). The two renaissances already mentioned, especially the Carolingian, certainly helped in the preservation and recalibration of Classical culture during that long seven-century stretch, but they have arguably drawn our attention away from the fact that classicism had been fully absorbed in vernacular culture anyway, and that it was actively manifesting itself at every moment, not least in the languages that people used.

Church-building was but one cultural activity in the period from 500 to 1000 in which the on-going debt to the Roman world was unmistakable. The whole trajectory of church-architectural development during the early middle ages had been activated by fourth-century, mainly Constantinian, architecture, even in places like Ireland where there had never been a significant Roman presence (O'Keeffe 1998). Even though churches sometimes appeared less and less Roman-like as time passed, at no stage anywhere in Europe did the trajectory of development shoot away from the basic Roman scheme. This is an important point that I will emphasise below.

Introducing Romanesque

I deliberately omitted the term Romanesque from the opening sections, although many readers will have sensed its presence. Cluny III is Romanesque *par excellence*. So too are the few other buildings I mentioned in its context, and the many others that I could have mentioned also: Santiago de Compostella, Pisa Cathedral (and campanile), Sant'Ambrogio in Milan, St Sernin in Toulouse, Ste Madeleine in Vézelay, Speyer and Mainz cathedrals, Mont-St-Michel, Durham Cathedral, and so on.

I will use the term Romanesque hereafter in this book. I will not present it in inverted commas (as 'Romanesque' rather than Romanesque) since that is tiresome, but I do wish you to read it with a sense of qualification, or with an understanding of its fundamentally problematic nature. By any measure, it must be regarded as one of those 'intellectual categories' within scholarship which, as the brilliantly perceptive Ernst Gombrich once noted, were created before their value 'in contact with the facts of the past' was truly proven, and which may therefore need 'radical revision' (Chaplin 1986: 3).

Before reviewing the historiography of the Romanesque construct in this chapter, I wish to make a very clear statement about the consensus view, already mentioned above, that church buildings of the eleventh and earlier twelfth centuries have stylistic coherence, and that the coherence manifests itself in the period's own contemporary-modern versions of ancient, inherited, Roman forms. I am actually not going to dispute any of this anywhere in this book (even if it may sometimes seem that I am). It is simply not possible to look at a collection of images of eleventh- and twelfth-century buildings from around the Continent and deny the general validity of those points of view.

But I would make the point at the outset that we must remember always that Christianity originated in the Roman world, and that Roman architecture provided the original template for church architecture in the West (the area that housed the so-called Romanesque in the 1000s and 1100s) right through to the later twentieth century. Prior to the Second Vatican Council, it was simply inconceivable within the Roman (Catholic) tradition to have a church building that did *not* follow to some obvious degree the model that was set down for Christian liturgical architecture between the early fourth and early fifth centuries AD.

I think it is a reasonable generalisation to say that, prior to the Italian Renaissance many centuries later, stylistic proximities to Rome diminished as chronological distance increased. Put another way, the debt to Rome and to its design template declined in obviousness as the centuries passed between the fifth and the fourteenth, with significant changes in trajectory in the period around 800 (when the debt increased with the Carolingian renaissance) and again in the mid-twelfth century (when the debt decreased with the appearance of Gothic in the Paris Basin). Detached from the wider model of a renaissance, the church buildings of the post-1050 period could be interpreted as easily in terms of *continuity* from the Roman past as in terms of a *revival*. Any assertion, then, that the buildings of the 1000s and early 1100s collectively represent some particular form of rapprochement with the Classical past must be tempered by the observation that, prior to the rupture that is St Denis, there was no other design system available.

While the tendency in synthetic scholarship on Romanesque has been to acknowledge the revival or reconfiguration of Roman form as the pan-European commonality in the eleventh- and twelfth-century building boom (as, *inter alia*, we will see in this book), I prefer to see the Roman presence as entirely 'natural' for that period. I have no difficulty conceiving of the buildings of the 1000s and early 1100s as a group, based on the fact that there was a building boom and a general climate of reform, but I am less inclined to see the collective of buildings described as Romanesque as ring-fenced stylistically or ideologically by its quasi-classicism or neo-classicism. We should surely be much less concerned with documenting or celebrating commonality than with trying to evaluate the nature of difference within the relatively narrow framework that the Roman inheritance offered to eleventh- and twelfth-century builders. If there is one failing in all the literature about Romanesque it is, I insist, that there is no theory of difference. I will return to this issue again. My book provides no more than a first step on an appropriate path.

So what *exactly* is Romanesque?

In the public imagination, the term Romanesque applies mainly, probably most accurately, and certainly most identifiably, to architecture. It is often described as the 'round-arch style' of medieval building. As very simple definitions go, this is not entirely bad. Yes, buildings of many periods used round arches, even in the period of the Gothic 'pointed-arch style', but those that are described by people-in-the-know as Romanesque do have round arches in abundance and are dominated visually by them. Contemporary objects of art executed in other media (metalwork, illuminated books, wall paintings, and so on) also carry the name Romanesque, but what separates them from comparable works described as Gothic is not always as obvious, except to the trained eye.

Whether we accept that unfussy 'round-arch' definition or, as scholars, seek or demand a more complex formulation, we can basically conceive of the term Romanesque as a very thin membrane that is stretched across vast quantities and great diversities of material. The corpus of objects or monuments involved is simply enormous. It is critical for us to understand that the term is not a neutral label attached to this corpus or to its individual components. On the contrary, as a term that was coined (as we will see) in the period of post-medieval romanticism to articulate a particular point of view about the architecture of the eleventh and twelfth centuries, it naturally shapes our perception of the architectural works, individually and collectively, to which it is attached. It is a core principle of contemporary critical thinking that what we purport to possess as objective knowledge about the world, past or present, is fundamentally rooted in and bounded by our cultural values, and is articulated in culturally-loaded ways. Thus, if we accept that complex medieval cultural values are embodied in the actual buildings that we describe as Romanesque, we must equally accept that the cultural values of the last two centuries are embodied in their characterisation as Romanesque.

To return to the issue of definition, we will see in this chapter (and indeed in the next) that it has long been problematic. The 'round-arch' style may suffice in popular contexts but is self-evidently inadequate at more advanced levels of engagement. Yet there is no definition in the specialist literature which captures essences of all those buildings and groups of buildings mentioned above, nor, *contra* Raymond Oursel who writes that 'son essence est théologique et théophanique' (1986: 13), is there any essence that stands out, seeming to transcend the simple secularism that definitions offer. The same is true of sculpture, *contra*, say, Pascal Soufflet's description of Romanesque sculpture as 'the material representation of Platonic philosophy' (1981: 5). Anyway, essentialism is a philosophical position that is hugely problematic, and any definition that invokes it can be easily countered. Ironically (and revealingly), scholars have found it considerably easier to identify buildings as examples of Romanesque than to define the boundaries within which they make those identifications. Because the identifications of works as Romanesque have been fairly effortless, especially for buildings erected between 1050 and 1150, the issue of style-definition has generally been excluded from the register of critical issues to be addressed in Romanesque scholarship. I suggest that such exclusion is ill-advised.

Having said that, I would not argue that, in the context of eleventh- and twelfth-century architecture, we *need* definitions (or, rather, better definitions) in order to advance. After all, at the start of this chapter I was able to present a narrative of macro-scale architectural change in which the term Romanesque was not used at all but which still offered a framework in which many hundreds of buildings across the Continent can be understood to some degree. But that last phrase – *to some degree* – holds the key to my point about definition. As scholars, we are not in the business of understanding these buildings *to some degree*. We wish to understand them as fully as they can be understood. What I am suggesting is that the issue of definition needs to be addressed because we have made it an issue by virtue of our retention of and adherence to nineteenth-century terminology. How we define Romanesque, even (if not especially) unconsciously, is critical to how we study the corpus of architecture concerned, or, more particularly, to what aspects of that corpus we study. Once we introduce the term Romanesque into our discussion of a corpus of buildings we immediately change the complexion of that discussion.

Historiography: the nineteenth century

Until two centuries ago the eleventh- and twelfth-century works that we now routinely describe as Romanesque had no such title (Cocke 1984; Bizzarro 1992). Italian Renaissance scholarship, particularly in the person of Georgio Vasari, identified these works as part of a broadly-conceived 'Gothic style', named after the Germanic people – the Goths – whose incursions into the Roman Empire had hastened its collapse (see Frankl 1960 for a wide historiographical reading of Gothic). Members of the intelligentsia of sixteenth-century Mediterranean Europe regarded 'Gothic' as the art of a long, dark, millennium in European history, book-ended by the decline of Classical civilisation at one end and by its rebirth in Italy at the other. They made no distinction between a 'round-arched style' and a 'pointed-arch style' but simply enfolded the two traditions that we now identify into their larger vision of a barbaric art continuum.

It is surely no coincidence that the liberation of these medieval arts from this negative interpretation was effected earliest in countries north of the Alps, far in time and space from the smug self-regard of Vasari's Renaissance Italy. Northern

Europe retained many medieval ecclesiastical buildings in the early modern period, despite the religious upheavals of the 1500s, and many elements of medieval architectural practice survived into the 1600s. Romanticist revival movements began to produce forms of neo-medieval architecture in the 1700s, recognising in the process that a distinction could be made between 'round-arch Gothic', or *gothique ancienne* as Félibien described it in 1706 (Bizzarro 1992: 32-6), and 'pointed-arch Gothic'. Evidence that there had been divergent trajectories of architectural development from one country to another in the middle ages, especially during the thirteenth and fourteenth centuries (as between France and England, for example), further encouraged the political classes of the later eighteenth and early nineteenth centuries to articulate their own particular politico-national and religious identities in architecture. Thus projects to save and indeed restore significant medieval buildings often ran side-by-side with projects to populate contemporary landscapes with revivalist-medieval buildings.

France is arguably the most interesting laboratory in which to observe how a post-medieval culture of 'estrangement' (a term used by Cahn 1969) from the medieval past was transformed, in the early nineteenth century in particular, by the realisation that medieval architecture was a powerful conduit in identity-formation. It was Gothic rather than Romanesque (as they are now understood) that first fixed itself at the centre of French national consciousness (Bober 1978). The dust clouds had barely settled following the destruction of Cluny when Victor Hugo established the Gothic cathedral as a French national icon simply by making the eponymous church the true hero of his 1831 novel *Notre-Dame de Paris*. Adolphe Didron's *Iconographie Chrétienne* of the following decade, a seminal art historical study which focused on the Gothic cathedral in its first and only volume, then gave scholarly weight to the idea of Gothic as the quintessence of God-directed medieval endeavour

(Didron 1845). Within a generation France's *romanesque* heritage had come to be as valued in its own right, as we will see, but the Gothic cathedral never lost its authority as national symbol, and it retains it even to the present (for a critique of its romanticism in France see Erlande-Brandenburg 1994). Curiously, while the Gothic style, both in its original medieval and its modern-historicist incarnations, was also conceived of in terms of national-political identity and religious identity in Germany and England respectively in the early to mid-1800s (Boisseree 1823; Pugin 1841), it did not retain its potency in either country into the twentieth century.

It was actually in the second decade of the nineteenth century that the adjective *romanesque* first emerged as the preferred name for those high medieval buildings that seemed to owe a direct debt to Roman architecture, not least through their possession of round arches. William Gunn, a Norfolk clergyman, first applied the term to architecture in 1813, popularising its use in that context with the publication six years later of his book on the origins of Gothic architecture (Gunn 1819). The French-language (also adjectival) equivalent of *romanesque* is *romane*, coined in 1818 by Charles de Gerville, a Normandy antiquary. He regarded the 'heavy and crude' architecture in question as '*opus romanum*, perverted or excessively degraded by our uncouth ancestors' (Bizzarro 1992: 144; see also de Caumont 1824: 539). De Gerville's term first circulated widely in the French-speaking world six years later thanks to Arcisse de Caumont's influential 'Essai sur l'architecture religieuse de moyen âge' (de Caumont 1824; see Bizzarro 1992: 132-49).

The link with language

Although *romanesque* is often now perceived to have been invented for the use of English speakers, it is French in origin and was used in pre-1800 France for other contexts, mainly literature (a *roman* being a novel). Significantly, *romanesque* and *romane* share an etymological root with *romance*, as used in the context of the family of languages that emerged in the eleventh century. In brief, these languages have their origin in *rustica Romana lingua* (spoken or vulgar Latin), so-named by the Council of Tours in 813 in contradistinction to the *Romana lingua* (polite, learned Latin of imperial court origin), the grammar, spelling and pronunciation of which were reformed (invented, even) *c.* 800 at the behest of Alcuin, the Carolingian scholar (Wright 1982). Supporting his argument, or so he believed, that *romane* was the best term for this rediscovered high medieval stylistic phenomenon, de Gerville claimed that the derivation or 'degradation' of the French language (and, by extension, other Romance languages) from its Latin parent paralleled the relationship of the 'heavy and crude' *architecture romane* to its rather grander architectural parent in Classical times. Thus was born the notion that the artistic/architectural 'style' was the correlative of a linguistic/philological cluster.

Perceived connections and affinities between art and language in general allowed the following generations of art-researchers to use the philological concept of grammar to describe motifs and other recurring elements in art in general (see, for example, Jones 1856). But by the end of the nineteenth century there was a definite shift away from seeing art as developing or degrading in tandem with language, as de Gerville had seen it in the case of Romance and Romanesque, towards a more metaphorical relationship: the transformation of one was increasingly seen as a metaphor for the transformation of the other, and the two processes were not tied together (see, for example, Riegl 1893).

That relationship between the Romanesque arts and the Romance languages had actually been challenged at the mid-century point by Jules Quicherat (1851). As well as insisting that they did not have homologous relationships with the Roman past, Quicherat argued that Romanesque was properly conceived of as a stand-alone stylistic phenomenon framed chronologically by the Roman and the Gothic. Whether or not we can attribute specifically to Quicherat the move away from the narrow linguistic model, it is clear that the linguistic connection was asserted less frequently after his contribution to the debate. Indeed, the later nineteenth-century lexicographic approach to the architecture that one finds in fullest expression in Viollet-le-Duc's encyclopaedic work (1854-68) represents an implicit shift from architecture-as-language to architecture-as-text. It should be noted, though, that the linguistic model was reactivated seventy-five years after Quicherat in the seminal work of Catalan scholar Josef Puig y Cadafalch (1926), and that it has reappeared several times since then in provocative commentaries by Erwin Panofsky (1960), Roberto Salvini (1970), and Wayne Dynes (1989), from whom the following scheme is taken (Fig. 4).

Classical Latin [CL] : Vulgar Latin [VL] :: Roman Imperial Art [RI] : Late Antique Art [LA]

[CL : VL] : Romance vernaculars :: [RI : LA] : Romanesque art

Fig. 4. Relationships of Roman to Romance to Romanesque.

The real rediscovery

The acceptance that Romanesque represented a self-contained cultural phenomenon in the early to mid-1800s was facilitated by the liberation and redefinition of the Gothic style. Gothic's elevation to the rank of high art by *c.* 1850, and the widespread investment in it of concepts of national identity (as we noted was the case in France, Germany and England), impacted in complex ways on how scholars in the second half of the nineteenth century regarded Romanesque, not only in and of itself but also in the context of the trajectory of artistic and architectural development in the long post-Roman to pre-Italian Renaissance period. While the claims made for Romanesque – that it was a tradition of originality and merit – were finally secured in the later 1800s, those claims still resonated less than the claims that Gothic was intellectually, aesthetically and ecclesiologically a superior style. The naturalism of representation in much Gothic art, the skill with which it was achieved, and the incontestable structural sophistication of the architectural settings in which and for which much of that art was created, generally appealed to nineteenth-century observers far more than the often imprecise naturalism, the combination of fantasy and abstraction, and the dark and bulky buildings that characterised Romanesque. It is arguable that parity of interpretative esteem between the traditions was not achieved until into the twentieth century and the age of modernism, an age in which the apparent *naïveté* of much Romanesque art could be rationalised intellectually.

France, again, is an interesting (though not necessarily representative) place for observing developments as the nineteenth century gave way to the twentieth. During his peak years of activity in the third quarter of the 1800s, Viollet-le-Duc had been attentive to both Romanesque and Gothic traditions in his work as a scholar and restorer, and in recognising the importance of regional diversity in the eleventh and twelfth centuries – 'chaque province, pendant la periode romane, possedait son école, issue de traditions diverses' (1854-68, 4: 162) – he presented French Romanesque scholarship of the twentieth century (see Deschoulières 1925; 1926 and Crozet 1954-6, for example) with its single most prominent *leitmotif*. Yet notwithstanding such works as Ruprich-Robert's magnificently illustrated survey of Norman and Anglo-Norman Romanesque, *L'Architecture Normande aux XIe et XIIe Siècles en Normandie et en Angleterre* (1887), the second half of the 1800s was relatively quiet in French historiography. There was, though, a blast of scholarly activity after the turn of the century, especially from the 1910s. Robert de Lasteyrie's 1911 *magnum opus*, *L'Architecture Religieuse en France à l'Epoque Romane*, is probably that decade's most celebrated work; although little read now, its impact continues to be felt (Oursel 1986: 95-102).

By 1922 Emile Mâle, the brilliant Sorbonne-based art historian, at last felt able to give Romanesque iconographers the voice that Didron had denied them many years earlier. In the process, he helped reverse an apparent identification of Romanesque with Protestantism (see Curran 2003) and secured instead its status as symbolic of France's special relationship with Catholicism. Yet Mâle found that voice only after he had completed a two-volume study of French Gothic art and iconography at the end of the nineteenth century. Indeed, in the preface to his 1922 book, *L'Art Religieux au XIIe Siècle en France*, he remarked that he had begun his life-long research into medieval art during the late 1800s in chronological reverse, starting first in the 'order and light' of the Gothic; 'had I wanted to go back further in time', he explained, 'I would surely have lost my way' (see Bober 1978: xxiv).

Historiography: the twentieth century

Despite his statement about Gothic 'order and light', there is little sense in Mâle's work that he regarded Romanesque in any of its media as a sort of warm-up act for Gothic. Such an explicitly-stated understanding of it had all but disappeared after 1900. Yet it is subliminally present in some early twentieth-century writing. Paul Deschamps, for example, characterised the story of Romanesque sculpture as one of slow, methodical and continuous progress towards an art that was 'more accomplished', that was 'nearer to nature and more human'; its progress was towards an art that only emerged in its fullest form, he believed, in the thirteenth century as Gothic (1922; see also Vergnolle 1978: 148). Even where the evolutionary significance of Romanesque to Gothic was not an issue, the models of stylistic development that were generated in the early twentieth century were capable of facilitating such a conceptualisation of Romanesque. Again writing specifically about sculpture, Deschamps proposed in 1925 a unidirectional model of development in which each step improved on the realism of the preceding one. While one could (if one believed in such models) conceive of such a teleology informing the shape of the Romanesque corpus of sculpture within its own stylistic boundaries, one could equally, by Deschamps' thinking, locate Romanesque within a larger teleological structure of style in which Gothic is the more advanced element.

Deschamps' rejection (1922; 1925) of Kingsley Porter's chronology of Romanesque sculpture (1918; 1920), in the course of one of the early twentieth century's big debates about this art, is partly explained by the predetermined nature of his model. It is significant that his 1925 model explicitly embraced pre-Romanesque art: he argued that the pre-Romanesque sculptural representations lacked naturalism, and that the Romanesque sculptural continuum towards proper naturalism only began when sculptors embraced the model of Carolingian and Ottonian 'minor arts'.

Paul Frankl's influential mapping of the evolution of the architecture in 1926 through three phases, Early, High and Late, with the latter 'transitioning' into Gothic, can be interpreted the same way. Cognisant of the danger of the uncritical importation of a model of organic growth into architectural-historical thinking, he opined that the progression was a positive one, insisting that the Early, Middle and Late phases he identified were not to be equated with 'primitive', 'mature' and 'retarded' but were generally stages of improvement that led inexorably to the technical and aesthetic achievements of Gothic (for critiques of the concept of transition from Romanesque to Gothic see Bony 1963 and Sauerländer 1987).

Later twentieth-century synthesisers of the architecture, like Conant (1959) and Kubach (1975), have shared with Frankl the idea of a staged development. To their credit, they have been careful not to shackle Romanesque to a teleological march towards Chartres. On the debit side, however, is the proliferation of sub-divisions in their syntheses: Conant identified Pre-Romanesque and Proto-Romanesque (including Carolingian Romanesque), 'earlier' Romanesque (including so-called First Romanesque and Ottonian Romanesque), and Mature Romanesque phases, while Kubach identified Pre-Romanesque, Early Romanesque, Mature Romanesque and Late Romanesque phases. Elaine Vergnolle's scheme for French Romanesque (1994) – *Préfiguration* (980-1020), *Création* (to 1060), *Explosion* (to 1090), *Maturité* (to 1140), *Ruptures et Mutations* (to 1180) – is far more elegantly stated but is cut from the same interpretative cloth.

Some twentieth-century trends identified

The sheer volume of twentieth-century scholarship on Romanesque architecture renders an accurate historiographical characterisation next to impossible. But some general trends can be discerned.

New issues about the architecture have come into focus, or older issues have come into sharper focus. Among them are, first, the relationship of Romanesque to Roman architecture as well as to Carolingian, Ottonian and other 'renaissance' architectures, second, the importance of ecclesiastical reform and monastic revivalism, and the specific significance of *l'an mil*, and third, the role of pilgrimage in the dissemination of the Romanesque.

Richard Krautheimer's seminal study of architectural iconography (1942) kick-started a series of studies over sixty years considering the symbolism of buildings. Many of them have concentrated on the 'imitation' of critical historical structures such as Charlemagne's octagonal chapel at Aachen, the original St Peter's in Rome, and the Holy Sepulchre in Jerusalem (see, for example, Bresc-Bautier 1974 and Gardelles 1978; more recently see Plant 2003: 49-51 and O'Keeffe 2004). Others have followed Stephen Nichol's lead (1983) and have explored architecture as *theosis* (see, for example, Malone 2003; architectural iconography and its limits are discussed by Crossley 1988). What is notable about most of these scholarly searches for meaning in the architecture is how, by and large, they have paralleled the exegetical study of contemporary architectural sculpture: many scholars regard a building's principal layers of meaning to be those invested in it by its patrons and learned spectators (see Kendall 1998, for example), and they rarely reflect on meaning outside (or, rather, below) that social context. This is in spite of the fact that 'as an eminently public art form, more directly affecting social and political behaviour than the other visual arts, architecture remains an ideal art subject for the application of Marxist and social-history methodologies' (Payne 1999: 297).

A greater number of regional and national surveys is available now than before, and archaeological excavations, most famously by Conant at Cluny, have added significantly to our store of information. Regional diversity was identified by nineteenth-century scholars and was a key theme in their work, and new regional surveys (most famously those published under the Zodiaque imprint) have ensured that it remained firmly on the agenda in the twentieth century.

Architectural sculpture

Twentieth-century research on Romanesque is also marked by, among other things, a significant rise in interest in Romanesque manifestations in other media, not least sculpture, to which I now turn. Deschamps, already mentioned, was one of the towering figures. Arthur Kingsley Porter, his American nemesis, was another. The debate between them (and others, of course) during the 1920s on the origins and relative chronologies of sculpture set the tone for much of the century's scholarship. The issue of origin has never left the agenda, and the works that they regarded as central to the debate on relative chronology – the *ex situ* capitals from the main apse at Cluny, for example – are still central to it three-quarters of a century later.

Although it was by no means his manifesto, Mâle's work had shown how the textual record in the broadest sense could be used to interrogate depictive or historiated sculptures, in isolation from their architectural contexts if need be. The rise of modernism in art provided a blueprint of sorts for early twentieth-century scholars to think non-judgementally about the more abstract and the less rigorously naturalistic sculptural art (again without reference to architectural context, if need be). It can be no coincidence that both Henri Focillon and Meyer Schapiro, arguably the two most influential scholars in the field during the middle fifty years of the twentieth century, had a track record in the study of modernism; Schapiro's view was that 'the key to past art is contemporary art, and … only those who respond to the new can judge the older works well' (quoted by Holly 1997: 8; see also Camille 1994). For most scholars, including Focillon and Schapiro, architectural context was actually critical to the sculpture's interpretation, and because the study of the architecture was formalist in nature, the study of the sculpture tended to follow suit.

Focillon, Mâle's successor in the Sorbonne, was the master of the formalist approach. He argued for deep structures in the compositions of the sculptor's art. The 'fundamental rule' of the sculpture of the period, he asserted, was its subservience to the architectural framework. He understood the sculpture to be both architectural, in the sense that figures were made to conform to their architectural settings, and ornamental, in the sense that the figures were composed and drawn according to ornamental schemes (1963: 105). Thus, in the case of the capital shown in Fig. 5, for example, the animals' bodies could be said to possess a sort of collective symmetry that is conditioned entirely by the trapezoidal shape of field, while their shared heads might be regarded as a device to create the volutes that articulate the capital's basic tectonic form.

Fig. 5. Capital from the façade of Notre-Dame-le-Grande in Poitiers.

Focillon's 'law of the frame' formalist perspective in the 1930s shaped the work of some the following generation of scholars, most notably that of Jurgis Baltrušaitis, one of his most famous protégés (along with Françoise Henry, doyenne of medieval Irish art-studies). Baltrušaitis's published doctoral thesis (1931) is the fullest documentation of the patterns that Focillon regarded as proof of Romanesque sculpture's spatio-structural logic. With few exceptions, though, the concern for geometrical schematism that Baltrušaitis promoted failed to survive in undiluted form past the mid-century point. One little-known example from the more recent past is Frans Carlsson's *The Iconology of Romanesque Tectonics*, a work that states that 'the totally dominating rule is that the Romanesque church-sculpture appears within the tectonic structure. The sculpture is not loosely applied to the architecture but is indispensable and constitutes the very church-building, i.e. is architecture' (1976: 156). It is arguable that Meyer Schapiro's criticism of geometrical schematism's core principle – that it 'reduced content [meaning] to a passive role' (1933: 283) – was the principal factor in the derailing of the Focillon-Baltrušaitis project. Hearn's more recent articulation of its flaws has kept it off the rails:

> [Focillon's] analysis of the development of Romanesque sculpture was purely abstract and unrelated to actual circumstances of creation. Ultimately, when he sought an explanation for change and development he resorted to the Hegelian construct of historical dialectic, moved by the zeitgeist. His synthesis of the history of Romanesque sculpture, then, precludes an explanation of how the sculpture was created within its medieval context (1981: 15).

Schapiro is the most interesting figure in the historiography of the twentieth century (see Cahn 2002 and Williams 2003 for recent evaluations of his work). Although he wrote relatively little about Romanesque architecture *per se*, his contribution merits special attention here. Despite his opposition to the Focillon-Baltrušaitis model, he was by no means averse to formalist thinking himself. But underscoring his most significant contributions to Romanesque scholarship was a Marxian conviction. His interest, as expressed in 1931, was in the art's 'dual character of realism and abstraction, of secularity and dogma, rooted in the historical development and *social oppositions* of the time' (1977 [1931]: 125-6, emphasis added). Five years later, in private correspondence, he articulated his dissatisfaction with 'bourgeois art-study, as a profession', claiming that what the study of art required was a Marxist perspective (see Hills 1994: 34). His classic, Marxian, statement is probably his 1939 study of the cloister sculpture at Silos, a work he described as a 'critical correlation of the forms and meanings in the images with *historical conditions* of the same period and region' (1977 [1939]: 29; emphasis added). Thereafter, however, his work retreated from such overt political engagement.

Schapiro's achievement was to combine conventional formalism with the sort of extrinsic 'biographical, historical and sociological' information (see Holly 1984: 24) that formalist studies usually eschew. It was a combination that may reflect the fact that he, alone among the major figures of the century, was not a direct or immediate protégé of any significant scholar, despite his contacts with many, most notably Kingsley Porter, a fellow American. Although echoes of Schapiro can be found in, I think, Michael Camille's work on marginal images (1992), it is hard not to feel that Schapiro's influence has been negligible: historical materialism did not develop into the major trope in Romanesque research that Schapiro's early work suggested was possible. If generalisation is possible for post-World War II research (and it is dangerous given the volume of work), it is that scholars have moved within the territory demarcated by Focillon's formalist concerns on one side and Mâle's iconographic concerns on the other, but have generally stayed outside the territory that Schapiro explored.

Historiography: the new millennium

The twenty-first century is too new for us to be able to discern general trends, but not too new for us to observe that little has changed, that no radical new departure akin to, say, the 'New' approaches of the 1960s and 1970s, has been embarked upon. On the contrary, the most recent work on Romanesque to hand as I write, a collection of essays on it and Gothic in the *Blackwell Companions to Art History* series (Rudolph [ed.] 2006), suggests disciplinary stasis. It is a most useful volume in some regards: up-to-date statements on a whole range of familiar issues; a valuable historiographical overview by the editor that updates earlier accounts (and parallels mine here, written independently of it); sensitive syntheses of familiar themes and topics (Linda Seidel on formalism, for example, or Robert Maxwell on 'the modern origins of Romanesque sculpture'); good bibliographies that feature work that one might not otherwise encounter. The list of contributors is a veritable *Who's Who* of stars in the firmament of medieval art and architecture studies, so one reads the essays as missals from within the comfort zone of established, authoritative scholarship.

But the volume is, frankly, depressing. Although almost all of the contributors come from within Art History, one has little sense of the broader debates about that discipline's philosophy and epistemology which have been raging within the covers of its most enlightened periodicals (*The Art Bulletin*, for example), and even less of the potential for any radical rethinking of the materiality of Romanesque. It is a collection that might, in many regards, have been complied thirty years ago.

It is a little unfair to pick out individual contributions, but one stands out for exemplification here because its title features a term/concept – agency – with which social theorists, anthropologists, and archaeologists have been grappling in recent years (see Dobres and Robb [eds] 2000; Barrett 2001). The contribution in question is the largely historiographic study of the 'problematics of agency in Romanesque and Gothic art' (Caskey 2006).

In brief, the dominant current interpretation of agency within social theory – that it is a correlative of individuality, framed in contradistinction to structure/society – is problematic for archaeologists. It potentially disconnects social actors and their actions in the past from the collectives in which we understand them to be defined relationally (societies) as well as from the contexts (social) in which they have meaning. A quarter of a century ago Caroline Bynum showed how this very relationship could be placed at the centre of thinking about the twelfth century (Bynum 1980), using the sort of language that is now *de rigueur* among theoretical archaeologists.

There will be an archaeological engagement with agency theory for as long as archaeologists seek methodological rapprochement between social determinism at one extreme and the relativism associated with individualism at the other. A contemporary Marxian archaeology that does not accommodate the agency concept, even if only implicitly, is inconceivable. Given the complexity and fundamental importance of agency theory in understanding the past, as well as in understanding the entanglement of the past *in* the present, the equation of agency and (élite) patronage in the 'Romanesque and Gothic art' essay in the edited volume is over-simplistic and misleading. The essay does at least begin with a caveat: it 'takes its cue from generations of art historians, and, like them, concentrates on elite patrons of religious art' (Caskey 2006: 194). But one wonders why nobody wishes to explore the full range of what agency offers. Why must every path lead to and from Abbot Suger and St Denis, and every opinion be measured against Mâle's, Panofsky's and von Simson's?

Rudolph's *Blackwell Companion to Medieval Art* appeared as I completed my text. I opened my copy half-fearing that it would negate my own project, but I actually read it as an unfolding validation of the project. It is Exhibit A in the case for an alternative critical engagement with the architecture that we call Romanesque.

2

Opening the Black Box

Introduction: add phenomenology and stir?

It is fashionable in contemporary archaeology to 'rethink'. Since the early 1990s at least, 'rethinking' has been an explicitly stated aim of many research projects (and the term has become so regular a presence in postgraduate theses that one senses that some students regard its use as a passport to theoretical credibility!). The term suggests some fundamental flaw in the conceptualisation of an orthodoxy that pertains to some body of material. It promises a fairly radical intellectual re-engagement with the foundations of that orthodoxy.

Of course, the outcome of rethinking is often less radical than advertised; indeed, I resisted calling this book *Rethinking Romanesque* because it stops well short of radicalism: a truly radical step would be to suggest dispensing with the term Romanesque altogether, a not unjustified gambit. In much 'rethought' archaeology the actual terminology of orthodox traditionalism is retained, so that the rethinking is contained within, and is therefore compromised by, the very framework that it purports to challenge. On close examination, the outcomes of rethinking are often no more than additions to, or occasionally reorientations of, orthodoxies. Add phenomenology and stir.

If we are to rethink Romanesque we have two things specifically to rethink. One is the 'story' that we write or narrate about the monuments that we regard as constituting the style. The other is the label itself, and its role in determining what is 'in' (places like Durham and Compostella) and what is 'out' (places like Brixworth and Laon).

Regional schools and Romanesque origins

The two themes that have most exercised the minds of students of Romanesque over the past century and a half have probably been origins and regional diversity. In a sense they actually comprise one theme rather than two.

First, as soon as Romanesque was identified as a phenomenon that varied in form and detail from region to region, the relative chronology of that regionalism, and the identity of its primary region (or region of ultimate invention), became subjects of dispute. Thus the claims and counter-claims of the English and French to be the 'inventors' of the Romanesque construct in the early 1800s are paralleled in the unfolding historiography by the claims and counter-claims for certain regions to be regarded as the inventors of the phenomenon itself back in the eleventh century.

Secondly, there is a view that the emergence of regionalism marks the actual beginning of Romanesque, since the conditions that are understood to have permitted its development in the first instance are the same conditions that allowed it to develop regional characteristics. Writing of the *arts mobiliers* three decades ago, for example, Peter Lasko claimed that

> ... a change of fundamental importance takes place in the second half of the eleventh century. Art is no longer created in short bursts of activity as a direct result of the patronage of enlightened, cultured, and wealthy individuals; it is no longer fostered, one might even say somewhat artificially fostered, by artists and craftsmen called together from different sources, arbitrarily selected by the personal tastes and preferences of patrons; it begins to

> take on a regional character. The growth in the independence and wealth of monasteries and of cities resulted in the creation of regional schools, the product of a far more continuous and more widely based local patronage (1972: 143).

Historically, Romanesque regionalism has been conceived of at two basic scales: the macro, comprised of northern Europe and southern Europe, and the micro (or 'school'-level), comprised of regions within national boundaries, or regions that traverse national boundaries but are relatively restricted in geographical area.

Early debates concentrated on the macro-scale. Was Romanesque an invention of the Mediterranean, the original home of the Roman tradition? Or was it a northern phenomenon, connected with the Germanic imperial revival of the late eighth century or with one of the contemporary and later northern religious reform movements? Northern European scholars, English, French and German, whose research generated and shaped the Romanesque model in the first instance, opted for the northern origin, sometimes revealing their own national backgrounds if not also their nationalist ideologies in choosing one country or ethnic group over another. The most notoriously ideological supporter of the northern-origin thesis was Josef Strzygowski. An early advocate of the once-fashionable *ex oriente lux* principle, which held that the critical formative influences on art and culture in the *occident*, the West, came from the *orient*, the East (1901; see also Corroyer 1888, Mâle 1917, Puig y Cadafalch 1928, and Atroshenko and Collins 1985), Strzygowski later soiled his interpretation by invoking a racial dimension (1920). It should be said, in fairness to Strzygowski, that invoking race was not uncommon in Art History; the not-unrelated belief that nationhood bestows character of particular quality emerges, for example, in Pevsner's work (1956).

This northern hypothesis, if it can be described as that, has held for most of the past century. It has, at different moments in time, carried imprimaturs from – note the surnames – Paul Frankl, Henri Focillon, Jean Bony, Louis Grodecki, Walter Horn, Kenneth Conant, René Crozet, and Hans Erich Kubach. An early, and now little-known, expression of it was by Jonny Roosval (1930), who regarded northern France and western Germany as the core region among the five Romanesque regions that he identified. Central to the hypothesis for many of these writers is that so-called Carolingian renaissance that we discussed in Chapter 1; this is adduced by some (Conant, most famously, but also more recently by Fernie) as an early Romanesque stage in its own right, and by others as the conduit by which Romanesque art connected to its Classical Roman parent.

In recent years, however, the macro-scale has been debated again, with a shift to the southern hypothesis. Josef Puig y Cadafalch, the Catalan scholar who was active in the first half of the twentieth century, is properly credited with the earliest truly informed articulation of the thesis that Romanesque architectural origins are in the Mediterranean lands, specifically in the arc of territory connecting the Po valley of northern Italy with Catalonia (Puig y Cadafalch 1926; 1928; 1935; for Catalonia see also Durliat 1989). Eleventh-century Romanesque architecture in that region still bears the name he gave to it: 'First Romanesque'; so closely associated is that phrase with the northern Mediterranean rim that we often forget that 'First Romanesque' features are also found north of the Alps (see Fernie 2006: Fig. 14-5). Roberto Salvini pushed the issue even harder in 1970, adding social-political context to the pro-Mediterranean mix: he regarded Carolingian and Ottonian art, 'art favoured by the Emperor and by the high nobility, a typical court art', as 'fundamentally and totally different from Romanesque art, an art which rose from the middle-class culture of the

Italian communes and from the similar social background of the by now industrialised French monasteries' (1970: 1); the language of Salvini's argument reminds us that the debate on origins has always been fundamentally political, with Salvini's own political contribution being rooted in Marxism as well as nationalism. More recently still, Edson Armi has argued that the fully integrated elevations that he regards as diagnostic of Romanesque buildings – piers connecting to vaults; external pilasters connecting along the wall-head via corbel tables – first appeared in the south, and so has argued for the southern hypothesis (1975; 2000; 2004; see also Lyman 1977).

The answer to the question where Romanesque architecture and/or sculpture began is, of course, entirely dependent on how Romanesque is defined in the first instance. If one excludes the imperial renaissance of Carolingian northern Europe, starting in the second half of the eighth century, then Lombardy and Catalonia, the homeland of Puig y Cadafalch's First Romanesque, step up to the mark. And so we end up where we started: with the issue of definition.

Now, the review of the literature on Romanesque in Chapter 1 steered clear of how the authors in question defined Romanesque (or not, as the case may be). That issue of definition is, of course, ever-present, but often silently so. When scholars choose between northern and southern Europe as the general place of origin of Romanesque, and then choose some locale within one or other part of Europe as the specific birthplace, they are ostensibly engaging primarily with chronology. First and foremost, however, they are discriminating (often without articulating it) within a range of potential defining variables. Sometimes those variables are purely design or structural: the lack of bay-division from floor to wall-head in the elevations of Carolingian churches, for example, might disqualify them from the Romanesque category in the minds of some writers but matters less to other writers. But at other times, it must be said, those defining variables are purely chronological, with sites disqualified from the category, or reduced to some nebulous 'proto-' or 'pre- Romanesque' category, because their dates are too early. It is perfectly conceivable, for example, that the palace hall of Ramiro I of Asturia at Naranco (Priego 1995: 169-91) would be described as Romanesque were it to carry a date of *c.* 1050 (which actually would not be entirely out of keeping with its character) rather than *c.* 850.

The point I wish to make here is that supporters of both northern and southern origins can both be correct within whatever terms they choose. This north-south dispute over origins is entirely a dispute over definition. The fact that scholars can discriminate in different ways to produce different 'truths' sets off the alarm bells precisely because both sides claim to have discovered the single truth about Romanesque origins.

Twenty-five years ago Eric Fernie experimented with the rather more macro-scale understanding of Romanesque, effectively drawing together, as others had done before him, all the variables or 'signs' (though without identifying them) into a grand Romanesque entity, a coherent pan-European style. Recognising that the period in which the variables first appeared was a short one, he found it difficult to choose one particular place of origin over another. On the credit side, he draws us away from that overtly political debate on origins discussed above; on the debit side he nudges towards invoking the Zeitgeist:

> The origins of the Romanesque cannot be dated more precisely than to between the first half of the 10th century and the first half of the 11th, and even then the signs appear, with an amazing consistency in their variety, in Lombardy, Catalonia, Burgundy, the Rhineland, Saxony and the Loire Valley, that is to say across most of western Europe. To an unreconstructed empiricist the concept of the *zeitgeist* or 'spirit of the age' is of little use in the study

> of history, but at least for the time being it has to be admitted that no satisfactory diffusionist explanation for this phenomenon has yet to be proposed (1983: 73).

So, is it real?

George Zarnecki opened his general popular survey of the entire Romanesque spectrum of art and architecture some twenty years ago with the plain admission that the word, or more particularly the concept, is indeed not easily defined. Impatient to introduce us to the actual material that is embraced within the rubric, he raced past this troublesome issue, devoting only a rather casual opening paragraph to an acknowledgement that it is an issue at all:

> For various reasons, the chronological limits of the Romanesque period cannot be clearly defined. First of all, they vary from country to country. Secondly, the Romanesque style is not easy to define and its beginnings, especially, are imperceptible, so that it is often impossible to state categorically that any given work is already Romanesque. Similarly, at the other end, the change from Romanesque into Gothic did not occur overnight, and the period of transition varied in duration from region to region. Generally speaking, however, bearing in mind the imperfections of any firm definitions, it can be said that, by the middle of the eleventh century, the Romanesque style was already firmly established, after a preliminary period of about fifty years, during which the style had gradually evolved (1989: 5).

This is an extraordinary and revealing statement. It treats Romanesque as a sort of historical *fait accompli* rather than as a construct invented two hundred years ago. It is a quote that is primed, as I have elsewhere claimed of it (O'Keeffe 2003: 29), for an intelligent student to hit back with a very clever question: how, given all the qualifications named here, do we know Romanesque to be real? That student could press the issue. If, close to its beginnings, 'it is often impossible to state categorically that any given work is already Romanesque', where does its reality reside? How can one begin to take sides in the great trans-Alpine struggle over ownership of the first (or even First) Romanesque in a context of such uncertainty? How, in our search for origins, can we confidently turn away from places regarded as peripheral chronologically and/or geographically to western Europe's major north-south axis – Constantinople and the Byzantine east, Visigothic and Asturian Iberia, the late Insular (or Hiberno-Saxon) world, for example – when we are unsure of the nature, not to mention the geography, of the style's European core? How, basically, can one be sure that in comparing 'Romanesques' in different parts of Europe one is always comparing like with like?

More recently, Eric Fernie has been even more explicit about Romanesque's historical reality. He is worth quoting at length on this for two reasons. First, his apparent unease twenty-five years ago with the notion of the Zeitgeist (see pp. 50-1 above) might have raised doubts in his mind about the Romanesque category; after all, any cultural category that seems to require a Zeitgeist explanation demands to be deconstructed. Secondly, he, unlike Zarnecki, seems to be articulating a defence of the category as if directly addressing the sort of charge that I have outlined against Zarnecki. In the quote that follows, the style's historical reality is a given, with the evidence being in physical forms and configurations that, in their description (see the emphasis added in the quote above), seem almost to hint at some deep Christian-philosophical homology of a type that we might find exposed in Stephen Nichol's work:

> [It] is worthwhile asking if the new style is a convincing historical phenomenon or merely the result of an academic exercise. It [i.e. the claim that it is 'a convincing historical phenomenon'] is supported by the clarity of its main characteristic, which is most often seen, in all the visual arts but especially in architecture, as *the articulation of parts from smallest to largest, forming clear geometrical shapes which relate to one another in understandable ways.* The early eleventh-century church of St Vincent at Cardona in Catalonia can be used to exemplify the style, in that it is composed of *clearly readable masses and volumes and has an interior which can be determined from the exterior.* Equally important is the consistency of the changes which take place within it, as for example with the differences between the late eleventh-century portal of St Etienne in Caen and the portal of a century later in the castle hall in Durham, two Norman buildings which illustrate a classic development from simple to complex. Patterns of change like these imply no mystical 'life' of forms, but rather the psychology of use and enjoyment, of boredom and invention, as such establishing that the masons responsible were working within a tradition. This evidence leaves little doubt, then, that we are dealing with a recognizable phenomenon, and from now on in this chapter I shall be using the term Romanesque for this restricted meaning and period, with uncertainty only over the date of the start of the period (2006: 295-96; emphasis added).

Apart from a brief but undeveloped foray into the 'mystical "life" of forms' – a clear allusion to Henri Focillon's work – this is virtually the Romanesque scholarly tradition in autobiographical mode. And it leaves hostages to fortune. Without meaning to sound facetious, does not all architecture possess, for example, an 'articulation of parts from smallest to largest, forming clear geometrical shapes which relate to one another in understandable ways'? Would buildings not fall down otherwise? By what logic can the qualities of two unconnected portals constructed a century apart – one in a Norman abbey and one in an *Anglo*-Norman castle – be judged against each other for the purpose of arguing some 'consistency' of change along the diachronic axis? How can one claim that the differences between them 'illustrate a classic development from simple to complex' and then deny this is the *vie des formes* in action? How, finally, can all of this woolly thinking leave us in 'little doubt, then, that we are dealing with a recognizable phenomenon'?

It is clear from the quotations from Zarnecki and Fernie that any problems of chronology and stylistic designation within the Romanesque category have clearly become ones for scholarship to resolve rather than problems inherent in the construct itself. That should worry us as we approach the bicentennial of the Gunn and de Gerville studies.

Roger Stalley, writing about the architecture, recently shifted the focus away from the word and the construct by thinking in the first instance about key themes in the architecture of the period, and then by introducing the term Romanesque within both that broader thematic context of understanding and the wider post-Classical, pre-Gothic chronological framework (1999). His approach, which introduces us to buildings through the prisms of such diverse issues as engineering, pilgrimage, feudalism, monasticism, symbolism, patronage, and architectural language, protects him from a criticism that can, I think, be levelled very legitimately at the two best-known pan-European surveys of the same material, those by Conant (1959) and Kubach (1975): the general absence of 'meaning' from the stories of architectural development in those two works leaves their stories without plots or explanations, and leaves them as articulations of 'the myth of progress' as defined by Olga Hazan (1999). And yet, while Stalley, like others before him (such as Lasko 1972: 143), properly recognises the inherent problem of applying the term Romanesque to a very diverse body of material, even within the architectural field alone, he does not attempt to break free of it. He uses the term repeatedly, with an occasional reiteration of the problem of definition, although his thematic approach would have allowed the corpus of buildings to be discussed without reference to any putative overarching stylistic unity. Indeed, both the content and the placement at the end of his book of chapters on the 'language' and 'diversity' of Romanesque architecture reinforce, I think, the idea that this material constitutes a single stylistic phenomenon, regardless of any protestation of his to the contrary (see p. 105 below). It also reinforces the understanding, present in the Zarnecki quotation above, that the cohesion of Romanesque is a problem for scholars to resolve with respect to the material, rather than a problem that the construct has had created around it.

On the whole, then, it seems that most scholars regard as unnecessary the prefacing of their investigations of particular problems of Romanesque with queries about the category itself or about the best tactics for studying it. Although the view that the term is problematic when looked at very closely is held by some, there is an acceptance that we know what we mean when we use it so there is no need to look at it so closely. But I would argue the contrary, on the grounds that any researcher who sets out to solve a problem of Romanesque that he or she identifies, and who then reflects on category and epistemology as *the first stage* in the process of problem-resolution, could end up seeing the specific problem not as one to be solved at all but as one to be deconstructed. Put another way, any of the questions that we ask of Romanesque material may be embodied not in the actual material itself but in our characterisation of it as Romanesque. The questions might be part-products of our tacit, uncritical, acceptance of the meanings that have been embedded in the construct of Romanesque. One could not suggest for one moment that the chronology of Cluny's hemicycle capitals is *intrinsically* unimportant, for example, but one could insist that the context in which their chronology has assumed such significance as to be very familiar to specialists everywhere should be questioned, and indeed one could easily argue that such questioning about canonical status potentially returns us to the capitals themselves.

Howard Bloch and Stephen Nichols, summarising the type of New Medievalism in philology that has yet to penetrate Romanesque architectural research, have articulated perfectly the danger of predetermined contexts of interrogation, and have even alluded to how the identities of scholars, or more precisely the 'subjectivities' of scholars' worlds, shape the inquisitorial emphasis:

> To what extent do our own strategies and desires determine the questions we pose and the answers we give? We cannot escape the obligation to clarify our own agendas. We can do so only by recognizing the degree to which the inquiring subject stands in a compromising position: on the one hand, involved in an enterprise that, since the Renaissance, has assumed the disinterestedness of knowledge, the objectivity of philological science; on the other, participating as a socially contextualised being in a network of predetermined subjectivities such as sex, social position, or ethnic origin (Bloch and Nichols 1996: 5).

The key point that I wish to make, not just here but in this book as a whole, is that by-passing definition is an option that is not really open to participants in Romanesque studies. It is not because we actually need a definition per se; after all, to argue that we need a definition is to imply that the construct is inherently a good and accurate one, a viewpoint which I am contesting. Rather, it is because the unspoken, uncritical, definition is problematic in our intellectual engagement with the corpus of architecture.

Romanesque sex

The astute observation of Bloch and Nichols provokes a slight diversion. There is nothing startlingly new in their claim that, however much we may desire to be objective in our assessment of cultural phenomena (whether it is philology or architecture), we carry certain baggage with us. Of the three examples of 'subjectivities' which they listed for philology and which can be appropriated for Romanesque, social position and ethnic origin are self-evidently significant agenda-influencing factors. The former registers in the sense of, say, Schapiro's 'bourgeois art history' while the latter is manifest in that trans-Alpine debate on Romanesque origins. Sex – or gender, more precisely – may be the least obvious of the three, but note how, of all the Romanesque media, it is the study of architecture, especially in its tectonic rather than decorative aspects, that has been principally (yes, not exclusively) the domain of male scholars for most of its history. Not too surprisingly perhaps (see Pollock 1994), woman are largely absent from among the names in the potted historiography on Chapter 1, and nobody could claim that I have censored some truly important names – other than Joan Evans perhaps (see Evans 1938) – from the pre-1950 period. So, how do we explain the 'maleness' of the historiography?

Sexual metaphors, both of masculinity *and* femininity, have been used in architecture since Classical times, as witness Vitruvius' invocations for Ionic (male) and Doric (female) orders. From at least the eighteenth century, however, architecture that possessed supposed characteristics of masculinity (ornamental simplicity; physical robustness) was regarded as superior to that possessing feminine delicacy or finesse (Forty

2000: 43-61). Thus it is tempting to suggest that such an identification, comprehensible within a Winkelmann-inspired historiographic tradition (see Potts 2000 for a discussion of Winkelmann's sexuality and its effect on his thinking) and perfectly encapsulated in the following quotation from Blondel's *Cours d'Architecture* from 1771, explains the historiographical asymmetry between the sexes on the topic of Romanesque architecture, which has always been regarded as a robust, frill-free style:

> A *mâle* architecture can be understood as one which, without being heavy, retains in its composition the firmness suited to the grandeur of the location and to the type of the building. It is simple in its general forms, and without too much ornamental detail; it has rectilinear plans, right angles, and projections which cast deep shade (quoted by Forty 2000: 47).

The historiographical imbalance to which I have alluded is one of two ways in which gender has been conceived of or has manifested itself as a 'subjectivity' in the context of Romanesque architecture. The other is as an *original* (as distinct from eighteenth-century) embedded presence in the fabric, spatiality and performativity of the buildings themselves. These two ways are obviously linked. That historiographical imbalance has its origin in some process of cultural exclusion, and it is not exclusively a modern one: Karl Morrison, for example, has noted how women are underrepresented in, and often absent from, medieval historical texts and image-programmes, and so were rendered subjects of male power, at least within those specific contexts of representation (1990). The corrective strategy for such exclusion is to probe first the factors that have led to it.

When communicated by the likes of Blondel, that idea that some buildings are 'male' and others 'female' looks like a very crude and essentialist structuralism, and is simply indefensible in our age of advanced gender theory. Yet the idea of gender-encoding in eleventh- and twelfth-century buildings has sufficient merit for it to be pursued more thoroughly than I can manage here. I can at least offer three observations which could form the basis of a more thorough investigation.

First, parts of the buildings were inscribed with gender-explicit symbolism. Gesturing naked female figures found in the allegedly marginal spaces of churches constitute the most obvious group, but, remembering that masculinity is also a socially-constructed gender category, we must think equally of registers of males, from prophets and apocalyptic elders to Christ, who adorn arcuated façades, portal archivolts and other well-displayed surfaces.

Secondly, given that the medieval Church was a predominantly male institution, and that the most sanctified parts of the majority of medieval church buildings were almost exclusively for the use of males, we could conceivably reverse the sort of argument that informed Maria Gimbutas's reading of spatially and structurally comparable prehistoric tombs (1989) and suggest that Romanesque architectural design, in common with other medieval style-design types, actually embodied a male way of viewing the world. If gardens and orchards in contemporary castles were regarded as female spaces because of their association with fertility (Gilchrist 1999: 109-45), it may be that the common positioning of more private or secluded female spaces – private quarters and private chapels – deep within castles, in places where access required penetration of buildings, was also a form of gender referencing.

Thirdly, traits of physical strength in the architecture might allude to increasing masculisation (as in primogeniture and the militarism of Norman culture in post-Conquest England, for example), but also to a compensatory desire to make masculine public and semi-public buildings in an age of 'a masculine identity crisis' (McNamara 1994).

Rethinking the story: the issue of networks

I want to return now to the principal issue of this chapter, which concerns the value of the Romanesque construct, and to turn to the 'story' of Romanesque that is presented in the various syntheses. It is important to acknowledge at the outset that, within certain terms, 'the story' presented is not wrong in any of those works. There is no intrinsic problem with the project of putting buildings into categories or identifying and sequencing the lines of stylistic communication between them, either individually or in groups. As an intellectual exercise the project of constructing such networks is valid and the outcome is useful. A simple narrative telling us, for example, that Building A in Germany is related to Building B in Italy, and that Building C in France was built later than either of them, may be quite a dull and plotless story, but it will probably not be wrong, not least because the phrase 'related to' is so vague. However, there are inadequacies in the methodology by which we construct such networks. Problems emerge when, leaping for the set of observations about the structure of the corpus of material to a set of explanations of the formation processes of its internal patterns, we purport to understand what these network patterns are actually telling us.

The methodology by which we construct stylistic networks between buildings is a comparative-analytical one, but it operates at very restricted practical and theoretical levels. There are three related observations to be made in support of this claim.

First, individual buildings are constituted of heterogeneous formal or conceptual elements in combination, and our comparative-analytical method requires that these be 'dismembered'.

Networks of linkages, such as those that are mapped for part of northern Europe in Fig. 6 using the narrative presented in one of the syntheses (Conant 1959), are usually presented as networks of buildings, but are in fact networks of selected parts of buildings. Thus buildings become *less* than the sums of their parts. One can trace the genealogy of such 'fragmentation' of buildings to, at least, Robert de Lasteyrie (1911), whose tendency was to split up complex works of architecture into different parts and discuss those parts separately within their

Fig. 6. A network of linkages in 'Germany, with the Netherlands and Flanders'; the narrative in the appropriate chapter of Kenneth Conant's *Carolingian and Romanesque Architecture* is here simply translated into map-form.

own typological schemes without reconstituting the whole buildings (his promotion of the idea of the regional school can be conceived of similarly, in the sense that it represents the fragmentation of the entire corpus into individual parts, conceived of geographically). The idea of 'dismembering' buildings for analysis is problematic, especially when the methodology does not involve reconstituting them as wholes.

Second, we operate on the assumption that, among the many parts (variables) that constitute complex architectural ensembles, the principal or culturally-significant ones for comparative study have been isolated successfully. Thus we give vaults and façade compositions, for example, greater comparative value in constructing the network than, say, joint-width in ashlar masonry or forms of pilaster. Interestingly, we probably rank plan-type highest among comparative-analytical variables, and yet, as I will discuss briefly in Chapter 3, the mode of representation of plan-type that we use is not only relatively modern but involves an abstraction of the architecture that would not be immediately intelligible to medieval builders.

It is a safe bet that not all variables had equal cultural value in the eleventh and twelfth centuries. While our privileging of vaults and façades over 'lesser' forms and details is reasonable, the relative values of such variables were almost certainly not fixed cross-culturally or trans-historically within our period. Can we be sure, for example, that details of ashlar were, always and at every scale from local to international, lower down the food-chain of cultural-symbolic significance than types of vault? The answer is no. In many contexts, cutting stone to the right size, dressing its outer surfaces, and then bedding it in near-perfect horizontal lines, may have involved as great a productive effort within an individual building as the making of a frame-and-fill vault, while the physical perfection of an ashlar wall, combined with its allusion to Roman work perhaps, may have given it a high score on both the sensual and iconographic scales. We cannot claim, then, that ashlar is of lesser 'value' than a vault, either within the one building or from one building to another, and yet our comparative-analytical method ranks such variables against each other.

Finally, our comparative-analytical methodology privileges positive links between buildings, but has no accommodation for what we might describe as negative links, those instances in which a conscious, informed, decision is made between two patrons or builders *not* to share certain elements. The methodology operates, in other words, a 'theory of comparison' without a counter-balancing 'theory of difference', unless of course one considers as an articulation of a theory of difference such claims as Fernie's about the differences between two century-apart portals being illustrative of 'a classic development from simple to complex' (Fernie 2006: 296).

It seems to me that the over-arching problem is that the traditional comparative analysis falls awkwardly in the space between a proper scientific method on the one hand and its opposite, which I would describe as a culturalist method, on the other (for discussions of the distinction between scientism and culturalism see White 1999 and O'Keeffe 2006a).

To elaborate: we depend over-much on our own mental capacities in conducting comparative analysis when such analysis seems to be tailor-made for the use of Information Technology. We (re)construct networks of connections using our memories and by consultation of images and published works, when in fact the technology already exists for these networks to be (re)constructed by computer at a level of resolution greater than we can manage by visual observation and recollection: just as criminologists no longer compare fingerprints 'by eye', so too can the architectural historian hope to deploy technology to compare buildings at hitherto undreamt of levels of detail (see O'Keeffe 2006b for a slightly different articulation of the same point). By using visual observation and memory we fall short of a proper scientific method. Yes, the argument against this is that Information Technology cannot be programmed to catch the nuances that we, who share humanity with the original builders, can detect. I agree. But I would also argue that we fall short of an adequate, compensatory, culturalist method. I would cite the inadequate theorisation of concepts of style, or the loose thinking that surrounds the deployment of such concepts as agency (discussed above) and architectural linguistics (discussed below), as evidence of this.

I suggest that it is a fiction of Romanesque scholarship that its practitioners manage, without recourse to Information Technology, to conduct successfully the sort of comparative analysis that is entirely appropriate to the material. I suggest that under-theorised concepts of style and style-change set the boundaries for comparative analysis at levels at which practitioners can operate mentally without recourse to technology, and so allow the claim to be made that such technology is not necessary. I suggest that the inadequacies of the scientific and culturalist methods basically feed into each other, one creating the illusion that the other is working properly. This is a theme that I pick up again in Chapter 3.

Looking in the Black Box

Rethinking involves challenging orthodoxies. We can certainly describe as orthodoxy 'the story' of Romanesque as presented by Conant or Kubach. To my mind, challenging the assumptions built into that story's comparative-analytical methodology, or arguing for the incorporation into 'the story' of a theory of difference, two issues that I have just discussed, do not in themselves constitute pathways towards a rethinking of Romanesque. Rather, they are projects that promise some refinement of the story without challenging its essence; they are projects for which the veracity of the story within its own terms continues to be accepted.

My point is that we cannot cross the boundary of radical engagement with Romanesque material and enter the realm of the 'rethought' simply by querying the nuts and bolts of the story. Instead, we need a different, even more back-to-basics, approach, and that involves, as the first step, opening the Black Box.

The Black Box is a metaphor. It is an imagined locked-up space (a box), the contents of which are stable and incontestable. The Box contains that which is regarded as no longer open to debate, whatever the field. It is the home of the fact, of the established principle, of the already-invented wheel. Progress within any field will *always* use the contents of that field's Black Box. Those contents are themselves so well established that they become a 'matter of indifference' (Callon and Latour 1981: 285). Even to conceive of opening a Black Box is to destabilise a field. Black Boxes are not opened. They are not expected to be opened.

I have appropriated the metaphor of the Black Box from the literature on the social construction of technology (which in turn borrowed it from cybernetics). That concept of technology as socially constructed is discussed in the next chapter. In this chapter, however, I use the metaphor without reference to its association with social constructivism or with the philosophy of science in general. It is simply a very effective metaphor for the point I am trying to make here, particularly because it leads to the additional metaphor that gives this chapter its title: Opening the Black Box.

There are two ways of thinking about the Black Box in the Romanesque context. One is to think of it in a twelfth-century context. Recalling the argument made earlier about the continuity of Roman forms in medieval ecclesiastical architecture (pp. 24-5 above), one could claim that the concept of *romanitas* was 'black boxed' in the early middle ages, and that it remained there until its metaphoric release by the Second Vatican Council. This is a deployment of the concept that requires a little more reflection than I can manage here. The other invocation of the metaphor is more obvious: it is the Romanesque construct itself that has been 'black boxed', with its reification over the past two centuries represented by the quotations from Zarnecki and Fernie above.

One of the possible barriers to opening a Black Box is political. Investments, cultural, political and intellectual, are made by scholars/inventors in the contents of Black Boxes, and so authority and privilege are challenged by the threat of opening. Some might argue, surely against the evidence, that the Black Box containing the Romanesque context has stayed closed for so long precisely because its contents *really* are stable. I prefer to think that the Box has not been opened because the vested political-cultural interests of the academy – Schapiro's 'bourgeois art history'? – have conspired to keep it shut.

So, what is inside the Romanesque Black Box? What I see inside it – others may see other things – are two misconceptions. The first is that high medieval *Europe* was a sufficiently unified place for there to be a common understanding of art and architecture. The second is that *style*, as historically employed with respect to Romanesque material, is a legitimate construct for unifying what are really quite heterogeneous art and architectural phenomena.

Europe

As I have noted, it is because scholars have accepted the reality of the cohesion of Romanesque as a stylistic phenomenon that they have accepted the challenge of constructing its history. But there remains the question of where, geographically and materially, this cohesion or unity resides? Although there are documentary attestations to high medieval aesthetic taste and to the contemporary sense of artistic-architectural inventiveness (Schapiro 1977 [1947]; Heslop 1998), no chorus of voices from the medieval world insists that we regard as one all this European material of the period 1050-1150, just as no medieval voices insist that our terminology must incorporate the word 'Roman'. So, we fall back on the material itself, and listen attentively to its garbled testimony.

Given that the diversity of the material as regards motifs and composition is freely acknowledged, both within and (especially) between the different media, the cohesion can hardly be claimed to be self-evident. So, is it actually context and date of production of the art and architecture – specifically eleventh- and twelfth-century Roman Christian Europe, as distinct from Byzantine Christian Europe – rather than its style (as conventionally understood), that properly constitutes Romanesque as a pan-European phenomenon? If it is so, why do we persist in describing it as a style, when that word strongly connotes visual attributes?

These questions have an import beyond the study of medieval art and architecture. Our construct of Romanesque as an international stylistic phenomenon implies a horizon of trans-national cultural connectivity across eleventh- and twelfth-century Roman Christian Europe, regardless of whether the evidence of other spheres of contemporary activity supports or contradicts it. The pan-European unity of artistic/architectural endeavour that the construct implies is actually more than simply stylistic: put simply, it signifies some common, high medieval, pan-European idea, or set of ideas, not only about the specific practical and political value of using Roman models physically to shape and give meaning to contemporary art and architecture but also about that period's own 'modernity' (for a historiographical comment on which see Melve 2006: 232-3). Crucially, it implies that the Europe in which Romanesque is suggested – the area that is more or less the modern, post-EU enlargement, Continent – was a coherent place, a geographic or cognitive entity across which a common intellectualism was possible, regardless of political, cultural and linguistic divisions on the one hand, and of the forces and facilitators of agency on the other. My own reading of the literature is that such coherence should be adjudged a fiction: yes, there was change in different cultural modes around the 1000s and 1100s – we are talking about a period of 150 years, after all! – but the timing and choreography of those changes were sufficiently variable, and their modes sufficiently heterogeneous, for us to query their coherence as a single over-arching cultural-political process. It is worth noting the obvious danger of circular thinking if we introduce Romanesque into the mix: we conceive of Romanesque as a unified phenomenon because we associate it with the twelfth-century renaissance, and we conceive of the renaissance as being unified because of Romanesque! The bottom line in all of this is, perhaps, that were it really so coherent, the art and architecture that we describe as Romanesque would be much less heterogeneous than it is.

Locally and regionally distributed traits so dominate the aesthetic of Romanesque art and architecture that, if we are to persist with the notion of a pan-European Romanesque, we are surely wisest to think of it as a quilt, formed of various contemporaneous and interlinked but fundamentally heterogeneous local styles, each with its own unique consciousness (and non-consciousness) of, and derivation from, the Roman past, rather than as an international style that, emerging from Carolingian and other early medieval 'renovations' of *romanitas*, trickled down as a coherent, ideologically-unified, whole into different parts of a coherent Europe.

Style

Style remains a severely under-theorised concept in our field. As with Romanesque itself, when we use the term 'style' with respect to what we define as 'art' we connect ourselves to a particular historiographical tradition of interrogating the interplay of form and meaning in visual culture. Style's historiography reaches back, past Gunn and de Gerville, to Winkelmann and the birth of modern Art History, to Hegel and his philosophy, and back indeed to Plato. So embedded historically is 'style' in 'art' that it is almost impossible to conceive of one without the other.

Hegel's profoundly influential Platonic take on art was that *the* essential truth – the Spirit, the Ideal – was revealed through it. Thus was born the notion that art was/is simultaneously conditioned by and representative of the Zeitgeist. For Hegel, art's unfolding history through time, driven by his famous model of a dialectical relationship between thesis (an idea or an action) and antithesis (a counter-idea or counter-action) was nothing less than the unfolding revelation of the Spirit (Wyss 1999). For a long time this interpretation allowed individual historic works of art to be understood as elements within a larger, Christian, teleological scheme, one in which outcomes are largely constant and defined, rather than (in the anti-teleological view) contingent and variable, or (in the Marxian telos) rooted entirely in the social practices and materialities of power and resistance. It is significant to note that Hegel placed the end of that teleology in the early 1800s, the same time as Romanesque as we now know it was being rediscovered, and that he identified the place where it ended as Protestant Germany, where the disappearance of devotional imagery from churches marked the point at which the Spirit no longer needed art for its revelation. Needless to say, it is a short journey from here to Riegl's concept of *Kunstwollen* (1893), where art is seen as having its own ontology and where the artist is interpreted not as a knowledgeable social actor with a capacity for independent thinking but as a conduit.

Today such notions are, at best, of very limited value. At worst, their ideology is offensive; one does not need to be a Marxist to sympathise with the youthful Meyer Schapiro's view of *Kunstwollen* and its adherents (1936). But they have impacted on how we see and read twelfth-century material and visual culture in three particular ways.

First, although more 'secularist' concepts of style have superseded the Hegelian (see, for example, Shanks and Tilley 1992: 137-71), the concept of Romanesque and Gothic as styles in a continuum that unfolds through time has clear Hegelian roots; Paul Frankl's work on Romanesque architecture in the 1920s, which implicitly invoked the thesis-antithesis dialectic without rooting it to social and material conditions of contemporary life, is one particularly influential study that wears its Hegelianism on its sleeve.

Second, scholars generally have rejected Hegel's notion of a Spirit or Ideal, but they have put in its place 'style' (in the narrowest sense of a set of visual attributes) and 'technology', treating them as if they, not unlike Hegel's Spirit, have ontological reality. To put this another way, just as Hegel effectively removed people from the dynamic processes that give history its over-arching shape, I believe that students of Romanesque have done something similar by conceiving of style and technology as autonomous, ontologically self-contained, phenomena that drive architectural change independent of human agency. I will discuss this with respect to technology in the next chapter.

Finally, the lack of significance attached to 'non-religious' art in the Hegelian formulation has surely contributed over time to the denial of the appellation 'art' to the craft-objects that make up the contemporary material culture of the middle ages. It has, by extension, widened the perceived gap between 'high culture' (represented by great buildings and great art, and intelligible to the select few) and 'low culture' (represented by craft objects that were available to everybody). I have suggested elsewhere, and still maintain, that this polarisation extends to the academy: there, the former is firmly identified as the constituency of Art History, where it is not really regarded as part of a democratic social domain, and the latter is associated more with the rather more down-market discipline of Archaeology.

> The evolution of a Romanesque scholarship so hermetically sealed as to discourage any social-theoretical critique of its subject matter is rooted in a series of loaded and difficult-to-break-down polarizations – art over craft, high culture over low culture, high intellectual ideals and technological achievements over the mundane – which the academy, descended from the medieval centres of learning, has successfully (even if somewhat unconsciously) promoted. In this perspective, Romanesque has retained the place set for it within the ideology of twelfth-century renaissance 'high culture': it does not really belong to the everyday, it is not a part of social history, it is more meaningful to the élite than to the non-élite (O'Keeffe 2003: 290).

To summarise, I suggest that 'the Romanesque style', as locked away within the Black Box in the nineteenth century, represents a view of eleventh- and twelfth-century art and architecture through the residual haze of Hegelianism. Embodied in it are Ideals, albeit ones rooted in the aesthetic and the technological rather than in the spiritual. I make that suggestion based on several interlinked observations on the historiography of Romanesque: human agency features relatively little in the story of its development; political, cultural and even linguistic divisions across the Continent are transcended by it, as if by *Kunstwollen*; it has an essence that only higher social classes can comprehend.

Defending the opening against criticism

I can conceive of two possible theoretical objections to my attempt to undermine the Romanesque construct by this pathway, and I wish to conclude by addressing them briefly.

The relative lack of published discussion on epistemology and Romanesque suggests that some – most? – scholars would regard as needless any rapprochement, either positive or antagonistic, between material and theory. Thus the claim might be made that the Romanesque construct has served us well for two centuries, allowing us to understand our material in a sophisticated way, and that any 'scholar' who queries its validity only exposes his or her own ignorance. But it is irrelevant, of course, that Romanesque has survived uncontested and unscathed while other fields of interest to Art History have been altered by the engagement of, especially, left-leaning critics. Could one not argue that Romanesque has served scholars well precisely because they designed the questions for it to answer?

Having argued *inter alia* (albeit implicitly) that the Romanesque category is undermined by its essentialism, there is a possible protest that the construct is not actually essentialist at all, since it is universally understood to be a pluralist concept that embraces, say, the neo-classicism of early twelfth-century Provençal architecture (such as St Giles-du-Gard) as readily as it does the stave-built architecture of northern climes (such as the churches of Urnes). I would counter this by claiming such pluralism to be a major part of the problem: how can one have a meaningful or analytically useful style-concept that embraces pluralism?

3

Modelling regionalism: technology and society

Introduction: three types of understanding

The previous chapter made two main points. One was that in the course of the past two centuries Romanesque was 'black boxed' and that the time has come to disarm it of its privileged status as the over-arching construct that determines how we interpret eleventh- and twelfth-century buildings. Somewhere in the past two hundred years the idea that this diverse corpus of material was a single stylistic phenomenon – 'a recognizable phenomenon' (Fernie 2006: 296) – took root, and it has managed to stick, despite its inherent problems. My argument is that we discontinue this.

The other point in Chapter 2 was that, thanks in part to the fiction of Romanesque, the study of eleventh- and twelfth-century buildings has fallen between scientism and culturalism. Now, that is not necessarily a bad place to be, as most archaeologists will know: the excesses of both – positivism and relativism respectively – are avoided there. But the problem with Romanesque scholarship is, I think, that the balance between the scientism of comparative analysis on the one hand and the culturalism that is embodied in the concept of style on the other has not been thought out carefully or critically: rather, one has been put (unconsciously and inadvertently?) at the service of the other in order to maintain the fiction of a unified Romanesque phenomenon.

How do we resolve this? How do we come to *understandings* – the use of the plural is deliberate – of the architecture if we eject the Romanesque concept and reject the interpretations that are pre-determined by it? Well, the answer depends on what sort of understanding we wish to achieve, and why we wish to achieve it.

I suggest that there are three types of understanding, each legitimate but each also requiring careful definition of boundaries.

The first type of understanding is a simple historical understanding of buildings, both individually and collectively. Buildings have structural and documentary histories, and the methodologies for retrieving these and for lining them up with each other are well established. Conant's work on Cluny, both in its investigative phase at the site itself and in its investigation of that monastery's cousins and dependencies, did not need to feature the term Romanesque *at all*. The methodologies in question are historical and archaeological in the old-fashioned sense.

The second type of understanding concerns comparative context and our desire to know, *because of their intrinsic interest*, how individual works sit within a larger framework. This is the level at which the concept of Romanesque has traditionally resided. We can explore that larger framework without the presumption of unity that the Romanesque concept brings to the table. One way of doing this is to adopt a rigorously positivist method, reducing the buildings to quantifiable variables and allowing Information Technology to sort out the patterns statistically. Yes, it means that we would no longer make judgements about connections that are based on our observations, but does that need to be a problem? If we believe that we have reconstructed by observation the correct networks between buildings (as, for example, in Fig. 6 above) then the scientific methods should hold no fear for us! Another way of doing this is by model-building, which involves conceptualising the ways in which different network-types might form. In this chapter (see pp. 91-3 below) I pursue that particular methodology, specifically with respect to the technological aspects of the architecture. I am conscious that I am isolating technology here, and so leaving out issues such as aesthetics and space, but my concern is with exploring an idea and methodology.

The third type of understanding concerns 'meaning'. This is an issue that I discuss here briefly with respect to phenomenology, and in more detail in the next chapter.

Technology, phenomenology and the rediscovery of Romanesque

It is hardly surprising that pan-Europeanism, and the regional patterns (parts) of which it is regarded as the great sum, was first identified in the 1800s at a national rather than an international scale. Trans-Continental comparisons of medieval buildings were more feasible in the 1900s than in the 1800s and earlier, largely for reasons of technology. The advent of a technology that shortened time-lengths in medium- and long-distance travel was certainly one factor, allowing scholars see major works in different parts of Europe, sometimes on consecutive days if they desired. The emergence of the technology of high-speed 'mechanical reproduction' (Benjamin 1969 [1936]: 211-44) was another, and was arguably much more critical. Photographic reproductions of buildings permitted scholars to see the architectural diversity without actually experiencing it in any phenomenological sense, as well as to analyse that diversity by juxtaposing garnered images of architectural creations. Allied with the contemporary penchant for making plaster casts of medieval sculptural monuments, as in the Musée des Monuments Français, they helped to generate what we regard as the canon, a canon being 'made up [not] of the actual objects but of *representations* of those objects' (Camille 1996: 198; emphasis added).

Photographic images represent mechanical reproduction *par excellence*; one captures in a 50mm camera lens much of what one sees at eye level when facing in a particular direction, albeit with some distortion. Other forms of graphic representation, however, fall more in the category of mechanical production (rather than reproduction) in the sense that, although they resemble photographs in being creations, or new artefacts, they cannot claim any semblance of the visual authenticity that photographs claim. The ground-plan, for example, with its conventions of representation (such as the use of the colour black to indicate primary fabric) is one such object. So too is the elevation or façade drawing, its vertical and horizontal lines justified so as to offer a perspective that nobody ever had, even the builders when they viewed works from scaffolding. And so too is the cross-section or slice-through drawing, especially that which seeks to explain through representation the invisible aspects of architecture, such as the downward vault pressures as counteracted by quadrant vaults or external pilasters and buttresses.

Although the marriage of these new artefacts – photographs and other graphic representations – undoubtedly revolutionised early twentieth-century thinking on European buildings, individually and collectively, it also edged that scholarship close to, though obviously short of, the generation and study of what Baudrillard described as simulacra, copies without originals (1983). In other words, the technologies (or mechanics) of production and reproduction clearly facilitated the impression, indeed the myth, that representations could capture a building's true essence for the purpose of its analysis. The multi-volume works of Viollet-le-Duc on France (1854-68) and Dehio and Von Bezold on Europe (1884-1901) are early examples; although the textual content was significant in these works, it was their images that carried the lexicographical and analytical weight.

I suggest that our synthetic studies of Romanesque architecture, of which Conant, Kubach and Stalley are arguably the most widely read English-language works today, can be understood as manifestations of the triumph not so much of the simulacrum but of the (re-)production. These books are fundamentally studies of buildings' complex representations rather than of their physical, ontological, realities. There is no doubt that the authors, to pick just those three, visited great numbers of the buildings that are featured in their works, and yet they have each written about these buildings in ways that communicate more effectively their knowledge of images of the buildings than their personal experiences of those buildings.

What I am asserting, in other words, is that these studies represent a tradition of scholarship in which original 'objects' (buildings, in these cases) are not so much mediated through photography as transformed into new objects by it (for a parallel discussion of sculpture and photography see Snyder 1998). The literary-discursive techniques in these books – the ways of writing, in other words – relate to the buildings not in their ontologies but in their representations or (to paraphrase Camille) canonical manifestations. Thus those literary-discursive techniques become strategies of representation in themselves, and the critiques of the contents of these books (in the review sections of journals) are therefore fundamentally critiques of writing, presented in writing themselves. James Elkins' general point that art history (and, by extension, architectural history) is 'in the writing' (2000) is thus, if unintentionally, reinforced; it is not only known through language and text (or by speaking and writing, in other words) but is actually constituted through them.

Reconceptualising the books of Conant, Kubach and Stalley in this way, I cannot help wondering if those writers ever wondered themselves what sort of return they were getting for their money in actually travelling to see these great buildings.

I myself have stood inside a good number of the great, comprehensively analysed churches discussed in those books and wondered what, apart from copyright-free images, was I getting *that I could use* that I would not get from, say, a Zodiaque book?

However enriching to our aesthetic sensibility is the experience of being inside a building, of sensing the warmth of its stone's colour or the coldness of its air, of progressing from a darkened nave to a light-filled presbytery and of observing the space 'open up' while doing so, our analytical framework has wrapped itself closely around those *visual* elements of buildings that we produce or reproduce mechanically. Henri Focillon's identification of architecture's 'unique privilege', for example, which is that it constructs 'an interior world that measures space and light according to a geometry, a mechanics, and an optics, which are necessarily implicit in the natural order but which nature itself does not practise' (1948: 22; punctuation corrected), acknowledges the experiential dimension of architecture but also distances it from the register of measurable, analytical, variables.

The physical realities of individual buildings, such as those studied by Conant, Kubach and Stalley, have so often been mediated through images that it actually becomes difficult for any of us, perhaps those authors included, to conceive of those buildings *except* as images. Sometimes when we visit buildings for the first time we conceive of them as images-to-be-taken, and so we perambulate them in search of perfect camera angles from which we might capture images of their essences, essences that will be studied and commented on from those very images. The academic is usually also conscious of his or her audience or reader: images are taken that might be used in print or in lectures, as well as for research. Sometimes photographs are taken to illustrate points that the academic has not yet thought of but expects to! Fig. 7 is an example of one of mine from 1986; it has taken twenty years for it to find its (ironic) context!

Fig. 7. A broken pilaster from Hedingham Castle's Romanesque great tower (early twelfth century), showing the wall's rubble core and a disfiguring down-pipe.

No matter how much we might desire an understanding of historic architecture based on other sensual engagements, the visual engagement is our principal one, trained as it is on the surfaces of the architecture (and incapable as it is to capture directly the spaces between those surfaces).

This emphasis on the visual has a complex genesis. In terms of historiography, it may be that the drawing of architecture in general into the embrace of visually oriented Art History in the late 1800s, not least by Heinrich Wölfflin (see Taylor 2001: 344), was the critical process, and one that took place at precisely the time that other possible avenues of cross-historical architectural interpretation – the psychoanalytical, for example (as hinted at by Vidler 1999: 485) – were becoming available. Romanesque architecture's continued presence within the purview of Art History means that its visual attributes remain exclusively in focus, since Art History remains a subject about the visual, regardless of any epistemological shifts (Powell 1995: 379-80). This would, as I have said already, be less of a problem if Art History's theoretical interest groups trained their imaginations on these buildings rather than leaving them in the care of arch-traditionalists.

Contemporary spectators in medieval buildings may well have been as in thrall as us to visual details, of course, but I wonder if our own near-exclusive analytical focus on the surfaces of historic architecture rather than on its volumetricity reflects two particular post-medieval advances: the emergence of perspective (and perspective drawing) in the Renaissance on the one hand, and of photography in the modern era on the other. Yes, it is important to place great analytical store in those surface details – bay-dividing pilasters, soffit arches, and so on – that are capable of easy representation by photograph and drawing, and yet one's initial sense when entering a building is often of its volumetric nature. That, in turn, fixes one's attention on one's own bodily space and corporeal identity:

> For the historian or critic of architecture ... subjectivity is as much the subject as the building itself, all the more so because the body is so fully implicated in the experience of an art form which is not intended, except in very special cases, to be viewed from a distance (Friedman 1994: 575).

Speaking personally, no amount of advance familiarity with photographs and drawings of the interior surfaces of Durham Cathedral – and let us be clear again that photographs and drawings capture *surfaces* – prepared me for the sheer visceral impact of its great blocks of contained space, or for the very particular temperatures, sounds and smells that were trapped inside it. Yet wall texture, air temperature, and smell may have been among the concerns of twelfth-century builders, alongside the laying-out of suitable plan-forms, the ornamentation of wall surfaces, and tectonic stabilisation.

Readers might be in broad agreement on this point but then argue that the problem here is finding a methodology. Do our experiences inside these buildings compare with medieval experiences, for example, given such factors as post-Romanesque changes to the fabrics of buildings? How do we translate what we experience within these buildings into meaningful data capable of testing at a comparative level? These are valid questions, but one can ask a question back: were we to produce maps of buildings in which a range of sensual experiences are mapped using isopleths, would we be producing images any more abstract and subjective, or any more conceptually or experientially 'modern', than the images – 'invented' ground plans, rectified elevations, and so on – that we already use?

James Addiss attempted a sort of phenomenology of Romanesque a quarter of a century ago (1983), based on that very belief that a more diverse sensual engagement with the architecture could add to our understanding of it. His work did not catch on and is now virtually unknown. His attempt to integrate some measure of the luminosity of interiors into the evaluation of certain canonical buildings was arguably no more than an extension of the normal visual reading of architecture, since the only sense that it invoked was still the visual. But it was pioneering given that nobody else (to my knowledge) was attempting to capture the sensation of moving through a Romanesque space and seeing it unfold. His study certainly fell short of achieving breakthrough, but that was down to a methodology that was relatively unsophisticated rather than a result of any intrinsic problem with his concept. In any case, its failure to generate a body of follow-up research had less to do, I suggest, with what he wrote than with the predisposition among scholarly contemporaries to reject on the grounds of subjectivity all experiential engagements with architecture other than the most narrowly-defined one of visibility.

Such rejection can be understood historically. There has long been a tension between different types of understanding – the Cartesian, the phenomenological, the symbolic/aesthetic – of architectural space and surface. Dalibor Vesely identified how, 'under the growing sway of modern science', a new fascination with 'encyclopaedism, taxonomies, comparative studies, different kinds of measured observations, and the like' profoundly altered architectural thinking and architectural practice at the end of the eighteenth century (2004: 242). He characterised this as a shift from symbolic representation to instrumental representation (what Aristotle described respectively as *poiesis* and *techne*). At the risk of misrepresenting his complex argument, we might understand it as a shift from a metaphysical and aesthetic understanding of architecture to one that is overtly technical and scientific. The susceptibility of the technical/scientific to evaluation by experiment, and so to some measure of 'truthfulness', gave it primacy over the aesthetic/metaphysical during the nineteenth and early twentieth centuries, both in the creation of new architecture and, especially, in the consideration of historic architecture. And it also gave it primacy over the experiential, in the sense that the aesthetic/metaphysical were, in part, experienced.

Aesthetic and experiential engagements with buildings as we understand them today can broadly be regarded as 'cultural', and the difficulty of measuring these cultural qualities in an objective scientific way has significantly reduced their value in the minds of medieval architectural historians. There is a scholarly squeamishness about such 'non-objective' evaluations of buildings, except when the contemporary testimonies of a Bernard of Clairvaux or a Suger of St Denis provide scholars with a comfort blanket (Schapiro [1947] 1977; Rudolph 1990). There is, of course, a false dichotomy between the cultural and scientific aspects of architecture, its representation and experience. It is axiomatic in contemporary critical thinking that what we purport to possess as objective knowledge about the world is fundamentally rooted in and bounded by our cultural values, and is articulated in culturally loaded ways. But the myth that there are objective truths that override cultural understandings of the world survives in small pockets in branches of the humanities, and I think that the non-acceptance of Addiss's basic proposition reflects that.

One wonders if the oft-repeated speculation that pattern books must have criss-crossed Europe, despite the relative paucity of evidence for them, reflects not only our culture of choice-based consumerism but also our reliance on the reproduced visual image as a mnemonic device. Could it be that the lack of *exact* similarity between one Romanesque building and another, even within the same region, reflects the store that medieval builders put in capturing essences other than just the visual? Is this where we position our 'theory of difference'?

The centrality of the region

Although it has not formed the basis of a challenge to the idea of an over-arching stylistic unity, regional diversity has been recognised as a characteristic of the Romanesque for the past century and more. From the outset, French scholars have been the most persistent advocates of the concept of the regional school. For example, the distinctive and exquisite Zodiaque volumes have been instrumental in the promotion of the idea that each *département* and *pays* in France has its own stylistic character by democratically assigning each a volume of its own.

The incontestable fact that architecture varies in significant ways from region to region in eleventh- and twelfth-century Europe suggests that regionalism is a valid model, impervious to the criticism that can be levelled against the general Romanesque construct. But the notion of regionalism cannot be divorced from that construct since the variation that is observed at a regional level is perceived to be within the boundaries of that single unified style: thus, the architectures of twelfth-century western France and the Rhineland, to pick two large-scale regions with dissimilar traditions, are regarded not as different in essence but as variations on a core theme. My argument is that these architectures may have a genetic bond, originating in the Roman past, and even a homologous relationship derived from the presence in each of them of local, 'pre-Romanesque' elements, but that such bonds do not make them any less different. To conceive of them not as fundamentally different but as variations, or as manifestations of regional variation/diversity, is to maintain the fiction that they are connected to a centripetal, or ideologically-unifying, norm.

Decoration and technology are the two aspects of the pan-European architecture of the 1000s and 1100s that most clearly manifest tendencies towards regionalism. The former, *decoration*, refers to those visual, non-structural, elaborations that are non-architectural but, because they are executed in stone and are constrained by architectural shapes and surfaces, are fundamentally of the architecture. It is striking how few are the sculptural compositions that break free of architectural space, or that seem to render architectural space subservient to them rather than *vice versa*.

In Chapter 2 we noted Meyer Schapiro's attack on Baltrušaitis's geometrical schematicism. Schapiro highlighted legitimately the dangers of a narrow, architecturally-deterministic, formalism in the study of the sculpture, not least on the grounds that such an interpretation as Baltrušaitis's presupposed that the carvers of the imagery were more concerned with composition (the spatial planning of images) than content (the iconography of the images). Yet scholars have never really deserted the type of formalism associated with Focillon and Baltrušaitis, and properly so. With the tacit acceptance that form is itself an iconographic point of reference, it has long been realised, for example, that iconographic readings of figural or historiated sculpture *à la* Emile Mâle do need to take account of the impact on image composition of shape-restricted and space-restricted sculptural fields, and in turn of the transfer of symbolic meaning to actual shapes themselves (see, for example, Oursel 1973; 1976; Cabanot 1987; Vergnolle 1994; for shape symbolism see Nichols 1983). Moreover, it is indisputably the case that many 'classic' Romanesque capital-types – voluted, Corinthianesque, or historiated – have tectonic forms, and this fact surely underscores the primacy of tectonic structure in the original conceptualisations of those architectures that we describe as Romanesque.

That observation brings us to the second, and therefore arguably more important, aspect: *technology*. This is generally conceived of in terms of the engineered qualities of the architecture. These are qualities that are semi-visible in the piers and columns, the vaults, the towers, and the massing of Romanesque churches; I say 'semi-visible' because the challenge of building technology is to deal with the invisible force of gravity. Every time we marvel at the achievement of the vault-builders at a place like Durham it is because we imagine their stone webs and cells to be defying forces of downward thrust that are not actually visible to us.

The issue of technology has long been as central to the conceptualisation of Romanesque architecture as its decorative or aesthetic aspects, even if it has not always been expressed as explicitly. Thinking historiographically, and specifically of the influential French literature, the achievements of High Gothic builders, the intrinsic beauty of whose work testifies to how technological success creates aesthetic product, cast a shadow backwards onto Romanesque technology in the 1800s. But, while that technology did not compare with Gothic in terms of tectonic daring, its own engineered qualities were far from negligible and their aesthetic qualities were immediately identifiable. The technological features of the architecture that drew most attention then, and continue to do so today, are the vaults and towers (see Stalley 1999, for example). That the focus should be on these most eye-catching features is understandable, but I suggest that the almost-exclusive attention that scholars, writing about Romanesque technology, have paid to towers and vaults at the expense of less sophisticated engineered components (Armi 2004 is an important exception, as is, in a sense, Eckstein 1975) reflects the teleological view of architectural change, given that towers and vaults comprise two axes along which it is possible to think of Gothic as representing an actual thought-out improvement on Romanesque.

Materiality: conceptualising medieval technology

Probing more deeply, the literature on Romanesque technology is characterised, I think, by three interconnected tendencies.

1. Technology is engineering

The first tendency is to equate technology exclusively with engineering, and so to confine consideration of it, as I have noted, to those aspects of architecture that required special technical skills. Technology, in this view, is perhaps not quite the same as technique but is conceived of as something more advanced: the organisation and deployment of specialised technical knowledge for the purpose of creating a target object, be it a tower or a fully roofed-over interior space. This take on technology is all right in principle but is slightly problematic in practice. Few members of the intellectual community concerned with Romanesque are really qualified to speak about engineering as a technical process (for a general discussion of balance between 'scientific' and instinctual knowledge of how buildings 'work' see Mainstone 1997). Like medieval builders, we – I include myself – do not have the training to judge the thrusts and stresses that a modern engineer can calculate or programme a computer to calculate. But, unlike medieval builders, we cannot compensate for our lack of theoretical knowledge with practical experience.

On this point, I once sat directly behind two architects at a lecture in which the speaker, showing a slide of the springers of a collapsed multi-cell vault, pontificated on the structural miscalculation that caused it to fall. Both agreed, in whispered tones, that the explanation was probably incorrect and that the vault was probably just badly built. I felt unable to adjudicate in my own mind between the two explanations, which is my point exactly.

2. Technology seeks optimal solutions

That anecdote brings me to the second tendency, which concerns the judgements that are made about the efficiency of Romanesque systems of technology-as-engineering. My point is not just that scholars assume a knowledge of how this sub-set of technology actually worked, but that they also assume that technological progression of the engineered type was always driven by the need to find optimal solutions to universally-known understood problems (see, for example, Bonde, Mark and Robison 1993). Social constructivists, whom we will meet below, would reject this hypothesis on the basis of there being no such thing as an optimal solution (Mitcham 1995). One of the grounds for rejecting the idea is that it is not impartial: according to social constructivists, the analyst should not judge the efficacy of a construction system, such as vaulting, so as not to soil the analysis by regarding certain solutions as rational or irrational.

Indeed, on this very point we can usefully appropriate to our thinking on technology Thomas Kuhn's original arguments about science (1996 [1962]). That notion of a quest for an 'optimal solution', implicitly present in so much archaeological writing about historical technologies, suggests that technological change is a continuously unfolding process, with one system of technology flowing into another either as faults or failings are identified and fixed or as new circumstances or conditions demand technological change. In his early career Kuhn would have disputed such an assumption of continuity. His view of science was that each scientific tradition possesses its own paradigms, and therefore its own notions of truth; it is a view that resonates well with the culturalist axiom that scientific truth does not transcend cultural truth (Bonnell and Hunt 1999). As a result, paradigms have, in Kuhn's thinking, a discontinuous relationship to each other. The shifts between paradigms are effected by agents with 'competing positions' due to their investment, political and otherwise, in existing or new paradigms. Substituting 'science' with 'technology', Kuhn's paradigmatic thinking offers a counter-approach to the traditional through-flow model of architectural change from, say, early Romanesque to high Gothic.

A Kuhnian reflection on medieval architecture destabilises conventional thinking in that it removes the glue of evolutionism, making all buildings contingent on more 'local issues' rather than keyed into a larger generalising structure. This is especially the case for Romanesque if one accepts the querying of Europe as a valid geographic scale.

3. Technology is autonomous

The third tendency that I detect in the literature on Romanesque is towards the de-contextualising of its technology from the political and the ideological. Technology is treated as autonomous, as possessing an ontological reality regardless of the social contexts in which it is used or in which it operates. It is a position that is not entirely dissimilar to Habermas's conceptualisation of technology (and of science in general) as non-social and representative of a 'objectivising attitude' to the natural world, in the sense that it has its own non-cultural life-force or (as Habermas puts it) 'lifeworld' (Habermas 1981).

Philosophers of contemporary technology have rejected this 'substantivist' (Feenberg 1999) interpretation with respect to the contemporary world, but students of historic technology have been kinder to it, largely because they can see patterns of technological change in the past and can conceive of them developmentally. The literature on the development of Romanesque architecture in general (and not just the vaults and towers) reveals this by implying a rational, goal-responding, technical progression that isolates technology from, and so transcends, social conditions.

Now, some scholars will argue that this is absolutely not the case. They will argue that developments in the technology of the architecture are *always* contextualised socially and politically. Certainly the literature on Suger's chevet and ambulatory at St Denis, an early Gothic example, could be cited in defence of this (see Kidson 1987 and Rudolph 1990). I agree that the end-products of technological endeavour – the buildings – are indeed so contextualised. I would insist, though, that the technology is usually conceived of as having its own telos, the forward momentum of which is identified as having being choreographed with, but is not being explicitly explained by, socio-political change and the concomitant need for symbolic expression. The evidence for this contention is in the language: the use of active verbs for the architecture, and the absence of people as the agents (subject) who effect (verb) technological change (object). Thus we often read that one building anticipates the design of another, or that one type of structure developed into another, or, in this example chosen randomly from Kubach's survey, that Romanesque develops through sequences unaided by human intervention:

> Pre-Romanesque architecture had already established the bases for treating the wall as something more than a flat screen closing off an interior, as a surface more than a solid surface. Early Romanesque architecture had gone beyond this and conceived the wall as a three-dimensional 'pane' with, already, occasional elements in relief. The mature phase of the Romanesque then proceeded to treat the wall as a plastic, sculptural mass, to be shaped and modelled both inside and out. As a third step in the process, the space enclosed by the walls no longer penetrated the wall from the outside in, in layers, but was itself hollowed out of the inner core of the wall (Kubach 1975: 145).

Theorising technology and modelling regional difference

At the end of the last chapter I suggested that we see Romanesque as being about fragmentation, about the centrifugal breakdown of classicism. Let me return to looking very briefly at how we might model such a breakdown.

Here I want to turn away briefly from the study of medieval architecture towards studies of the philosophy and sociology of science and technology. Of specific interest to my argument here is the set of approaches that are described under the term *social constructivism*, a complex system of thinking which, when it emerged in its fullest form in the mid-1980s, manifested itself in two closely related approaches: the social construction of technology (SCOT), and actor-network theory (ANT). Although the integrity of the approach has dissipated somewhat since then, it is that original formulation that I wish to use here (Bijker, Hughes and Pinch 1987; Bijker and Law 1992; Law 1991; Bijker 1994). Social constructivism's core principle is best articulated in the SCOT literature: technology is *always* socially-constructed. It does not exist except as a social formulation. It has no ontological reality, no autonomous existence, and no intrinsic qualities or properties. Technological change has no internal logic, submits to no telos, and conducts no search for optimal solutions to any problem. It is purely a socially-contingent process, involving individual and collective agency, and it exploits the heterogeneity of the social realm. Stable technologies are technologies that have been adjudged stable; technologies can not stabilise themselves.

In both ANT and SCOT the concept of the 'artefact type' is deployed, and I will use that phrase here because its flexibility is useful. It can be understood to represent a building or a part of a building, and those are the meanings that I see for it here, but it can also (especially in ANT) be used to refer to an idea.

Turning first to ANT, Bruno Latour and Michel Callon, the two principal architects of the theory in the 1980s, constructed a model that explains in an abstract way how networks or connectivities are built up and lead to the stabilisation (actually, the 'black boxing') of technologies. Adapting their model and its terminology to our needs, we could, by setting our dial to the year AD 1000, map abstractly a process to explain the stabilisation of any single regional 'school' in the early 1000s:

Problematisation

Dominant (political) actors create the impetus for a new 'artefact type' to represent the polity and their position in it. Through experimentation with form, they raise the issue of how that 'artefact type' should appear: for example, they are conscious that, in the case of our architecture, the display of *romanitas* is critical to the political project, but also that its display needs (a) to be intelligible to the audience, and (b) not to be *so* radical a departure from what already exists that it cannot find acceptability.

'Interessement'
Other actors, already politically-engaged or potentially so, become interested in the project of designing the 'artefact type'.

Enrolment
Those other actors 'sign up' to the new, emerging, vision of the 'artefact type', knowing that that they are also signing up to the polity that it represents.

Inscription
The 'artefact type' is now regarded as having been 'generated'. The political thinking is regarded as inscribed within it. The type is not neutral but is understood by participants or actors to communicate, and even to protect, their interests.

Irreversibility
The 'artefact type' is now so well-established within a socio-political context that alternatives are not entertained. It is not possible for participants in this network to step back to the stage of *Problematisation* and to proceed in a different direction, such has been the investment in the 'artefact type' and the scale of recognition of its efficacy. But it is possible for other actors outside the network (or 'resistant' actors within the network) to begin a new cycle of development by taking the *Irreversibility* of one 'artefact type' as the point for *Problematisation* for another: this is, in Kuhnian terms, the point of paradigm shift.

Like all such models, this particular model weakens somewhat on contact with facts, but it is offered as a way of thinking about process and politics in architectural change; it is an attempt at a positivist methodology that does not challenge the veracity of culturalist thinking about the buildings in question. One could elaborate on it by suggesting that in our context of Romanesque the first stage, *Problematisation*, was located within a core part or core parts of Europe, that the subsequent phases devolved gradually and in complex ways to local arenas, all of them at different scales, and that the regional variability that we observe is explained by that. One might even suggest that the well-attested problems of dating the start of Romanesque are rooted in the fact that different scholars are actually focusing on different phases in this process. Which phase might Zarnecki have been referring to when he said that Romanesque's 'beginnings, especially, are imperceptible, so that it is often impossible to state categorically that any given work is already Romanesque' (1989: 5)?

The model can be improved, and my suggestion of centrifugalism incorporated better into it, by drawing from the other social constructivist approach, SCOT. At that stage between *Problematisation* and *'Interessement'* new 'artefact types' can have what Wiebe Bijker described as *Interpretive Flexibility*. Artefact types will work (or not, as the case may be) according to who uses them and how they are used. They can develop *Multi-Dimensionally*, which means that each of them can assume more than one basic form or manifestation. Relevant social groups can interpret and redefine artefacts as they adapt them to their purposes, especially in response to artefact types that they already know and use.

In Bijker's vision, each artefact type generates, both around itself and the social groups that use it, a *Technological Frame*. This is a complex metaphoric space in the model in which a diverse range of issues and attributes is housed as 'goals, problem-solving strategies, current theories, tacit knowledge, testing procedures, design methods, exemplary artifacts' and so on. For our purposes, we might regard such a *Technological Frame* as being in a sense equivalent to the phases of *Enrolment* and *Inscription* in ANT, and perhaps also to what Kuhn described as a *Technological Paradigm*.

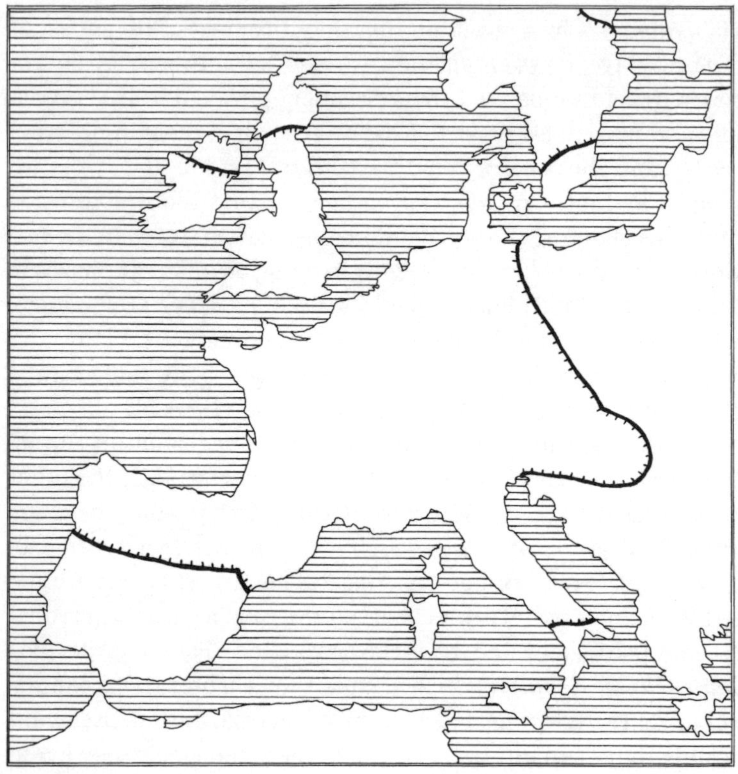

Fig. 8. Two maps of Romanesque Europe: *above*: the perspective that yields a single style and suggests a common vision; *opposite*: the perspective that suggests a multiplicity of styles.

Whereas ANT indicates that artefact types move from here towards a kind of irreversibility, in SCOT it is recognised that the *Technological Frame* will change according to 'social impact'. The forms and interpretations of the artefact will *Stabilise*, however, when the relevant social groups (or, as ANT people put it, the actant-networks), reach consensus about the form, or as one group's interpretation dominates. Once an artefact has stabilised, it is difficult to change.

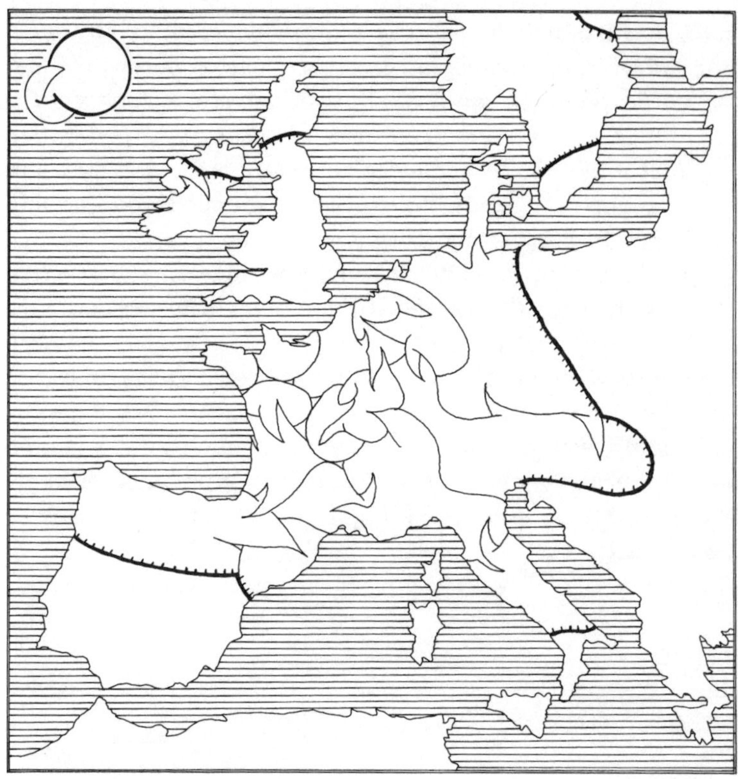

Interpretative flexibility is significantly reduced. It eventually arrives at closure.

This run-though social constructivism seems rather abstract, but the principles can be adopted to conceive of a generalised, model of the development of regionalism as a manifestation of centrifugal forces. This model adumbrates general principles by virtue of the fact that it is no more than a model, with change described (for convenience here) along a single diachronic axis:

(a) the differential survival of Roman forms through to the ninth century;

(b) a variable spatial and chronological distribution of *Problematisations* (as different parts of Europe rethink the political value of their architecture between the ninth and eleventh centuries), leading to the generation of different *Technological Frames*, as these issues are worked out according to their regional traditions and points of dispute are resolved;

(c) eventual *Stabilisations*, sometimes involving interaction with other *Technological Frames*, and *Closures*.

The map of Romanesque Europe that is formed by the processes modelled here looks from one angle (Fig. 8, *left*) to be a map of a single stylistic phenomenon, intelligible in terms of a shared pan-European vision of *romanitas*. It looks from another angle (Fig 8, *right*) to be something quite different and altogether more realistic.

4

Discourse and translation: domains of meaning

Introduction: talking style

In Chapter 3 the metaphor of the Black Box was used to introduce the particular Hegelian understanding of the idea of style that, consciously or unconsciously, has been close to the heart, I suggest, of both the conceptualisation of Romanesque as a pan-European phenomenon and the development of its historiography.

Less essentialist in nature and less ideologically-rooted in origin is the type of understanding of the idea of style adopted by Ernst Gombrich and Meyer Schapiro. The former, who was virulently opposed to the idea of the Zeitgeist, regarded style as a visually manifest mode of expression in which individual and collective ideas are held and distributed. He believed that style works by setting up 'a horizon of expectation, a mental set, which registers deviations and modifications with exaggerated sensitivity' (1960: 53). Schapiro saw it as 'a system of forms with a quality and a meaningful expression through which the personality of the artist and the broad outlook of a group are visible' (1994 [1962]: 51).

Of course, neither of these formulations is beyond criticism; the problem of how we actually rank the forms within Schapiro's 'system of forms' for the purpose of identifying style-groups will not be solved by either, nor will the problem of style-nomenclature. But these characterisations of style do, usefully, edge us towards an understanding of it as a trait that is, or is potentially, discursive. In other words, style is not something that works of art and architecture *passively* possess but is an *active* quality in how these works function within social and political domains. I will argue here that we discard the view that architecture ('Romanesque' or otherwise) works as language, and that we can re-imagine style to be an agent of discourse, one that is trans-historical and invites us to consider how the history of architecture is less a history of forms, which are static, than of meanings, which are ever-changing.

Romanesque and *Romana lingua*

On the issue of language, we noted in Chapter 1 that a relationship between architecture of *c.* 1100 and the Romance language family was postulated in the early nineteenth century. That relationship was viewed in homological terms, their comparability being identified in their parallel genealogical descents, or devolutions, from parent forms in Antiquity. Theoreticians from both fields – architectural (and architectural-historical) studies and linguistics – would probably regard as moderately sophisticated for its time the model that was presented (by de Gerville in particular).

In making the claim for a connection, de Gerville arguably made the wrong linguistic choice. If the great churches of the allegedly mature phase of *c.* 1080-1140 are to be thought of as homologous with one of the two standards of Latin identified after the Carolingian period, it is surely with *Romana lingua.* The regularity of architectural form can potentially be thought of as a product of the same ideology that regularised Latin grammar and orthography in the ninth century and later, and especially in the twelfth century.

There is another parallel between Romanesque, as historically conceived, and *Romana lingua.* Latin was really a second language in the middle ages, acquired by people whose vernacular tongues were Romance or Germanic. The proper spoken use of Latin, when delivered in the appropriate context, was an indicator of status: a fluent Latin communicator was educated, and would have been well-connected within the contemporary Christian intellectual milieu because Latin language and literacy were part of Church culture. One might argue that, metaphorically speaking, 'Romanesque' developed like a second language too, in that the forms of architectural structure and design that we encounter for the first time in the late 1000s and early 1100s were new stabilisations that built on but also muscled out more deeply rooted vernacular traditions. It is interesting in this context to reflect on the observation, made by socio-linguists, that speakers sometimes change linguistic formulations as different situations or circumstances demand (Fishman 1965). Just as we can imagine a twelfth-century cleric passing through ordination and switching from the vernacular tongue of his birth and upbringing to Latin, we can imagine patrons effecting parallel shifts away from their own vernacular building traditions towards a style or styles in which *romanitas* was suddenly more strongly in evidence than previously.

The relationship of Latin to 'Romanesque' extends from language-as-spoken to language-as-written. Both the twelfth-century interest in the actual translation of ancient Latin texts and the desire among twelfth-century writers to improve or 'modernise' the quality of written (and spoken) Latin in contemporary élite circles (see Martin 1982) can also be seen to have general correlatives in the architecture. One could argue that the neo-Roman façade of St Gilles-du-Gard, to pick an obvious if rather extreme example, is a parallel of sorts for, say, Hildebert of Lavardin's poem about Rome: both works are fundamentally of the twelfth century, since only in that century could such seemingly-slavish imitations of classicism be produced and still seem to be absolutely contemporary to their high medieval context of production.

Structuralism and poststructuralism: architecture and linguistic theory

Linguistics has featured in the historiography of Romanesque right from the outset. Sometimes it is a very explicit presence, with scholars writing about the style's language or grammar. More often the presence is implied in the methodology. If one were to identify the most common theoretical perspective adopted by scholars of Romanesque since the 1800s it would probably be structuralism. This has its roots in Saussurean linguistic theory, specifically semiology, the study of systems of signs, of signifiers and signifieds; semiology 'aims to take in any system of signs, whatever their substance and limits; images, gestures, musical sounds, objects, and the complex associations of all of these, which form the content of ritual, convention or public entertainment: these constitute, if not languages, at least systems of signification' (Barthes 1967: 9).

I have indicated in this book that Romanesque scholarship has resisted adopting explicitly-articulated theoretical positions, and so I would assert here that the scholarship's adoption of a low-level structuralism is, with some exceptions (Wirth 1989; 1999), relatively unconscious; it says rather less about the adventurous spirit of Romanesque scholarship than it does about the nature of architecture as a phenomenon that invites structuralist-type interpretation. I will argue here that the field's rootedness in low-level structuralist thinking has contributed to its limited interpretative capacity.

The most common conceptualisation of the language-architecture relationship in general – let us leave Romanesque to one side for the present – holds the latter to possess, or to be an example of, the former (Summerson 1963; Gloag 1975). In other words, architecture is understood to possess language, or it is understood to be a language. It goes without saying that we need to be very careful here. On a superficial level one can see the attraction of such thinking. As languages comprise words, sequences of words, and rules of grammar, buildings comprise individual elements arranged in sequences and locked into structural rules; just as language cannot make sense if its words are randomly arranged, buildings cannot stand up if their elements are randomly assembled. Also, we talk about 'reading' buildings (and certainly plans of buildings), we talk of surfaces being 'articulated', and we use an alphabetical system (albeit usually just A and B) to describe the rhythms of piers and columns.

Whatever we claim about architecture working like a language, we cannot claim it to be a language, at least in any conventional understanding of that word. If one of the functions of language as a social practice is to enlarge our capacity for communication, at least to the level of dialogue, architecture does not possess it. Buildings do not hear what we say to them, and they do not talk back. One is reminded of the old comic-book cartoon depicting an alien landing on Earth, walking up to a petrol pump, and asking to be taken to its leader. Moreover, language allows us understand things that are not 'of language' itself: whether we regard it as merely the tool by which observations and thoughts are articulated, or (as many theoreticians would insist) as part of the ontology of observation and thought, our experience of language is that it mediates in social interactions but is rarely the actual object of those interactions. By contrast, the only language a building can possess, even using the most generous understanding of 'language', is, arguably, an entirely self-referential one. Yes, the structures and appearances of buildings can be *interpreted* metaphorically, and symbolic or iconographic interpretations of medieval buildings in particular usually involve the notion of metaphor, even if scholars tend not to use that term, but I would argue that architecture, unlike language, is not coded by any intra-culturally understood system of signs to communicate anything extrinsic to itself.

In possessing discrete, identifiable, visual elements (signs), in having those elements (signs) work in visually recurring spatial sequences or as parts of visually attestable structural interdependencies, and in requiring those elements (signs) to be 'read' rather than listened to in order to be comprehended, architecture is arguably closer to text than to language. If we think historiographically, and I insist throughout this book that such a perspective is critical, the connection with text has been an important one. It has undoubtedly shaped Romanesque scholarship's dominant structuralist paradigm. Let me explain by using a simple model.

Stage 1

The scholars who comprise the 'interpretative community' (Fish 1980) for Romanesque have tended to comprehend its architecture textually (albeit implicitly so), probing its deep structures in search of its organising or defining principles, and thinking narratologically about its programmatic architectural figure sculpture. The by-passing of the potential referential meanings of the architecture and the non-figural sculpture signals clearly the structuralist nature of enquiry: structuralism is more concerned with signifiers than with signifieds; it is more concerned with form than with content.

Stages 2 and 3

This scholarly engagement leads, in turn, to its own textual production (Stage 2) and that in turn is subject to textual analysis (Stage 3); in other words, these readings are translated into narrative forms (books, papers, lectures), these narratives are then presented as scientific analyses of the signs and sign-complexes that comprise buildings, and then, finally, as texts themselves, the narratives are open to interrogation. At this point there is a feedback loop to Stage 1, as disputed points are resolved by re-engagement with the architecture using the same investigative strategy.

Stage 4

The interrogation of text-form argument in Stage 3 can feed-back to the buildings, as I have said, but equally the arguments can be analysed on their own merits, found wanting, and deconstructed. By deconstructing the arguments we feedback to the buildings and view them in an entirely different way.

I argued earlier that the creation of the regional groups of buildings that are lumped together under the title Romanesque resulted from *stabilisations* of different dominant technologies and, by extension, of dominant meanings. The key difficulty with structuralist thinking in the context of Romanesque is not its promotion of a dominant meaning at the point of building construction but its incapacity to allow that meanings can change, even without physical alteration to fabric. Romanesque architectural scholarship, which concentrates solely on the process of construction, privileges meanings that it believes were invested by the patrons or builders. It does not concern itself with phases of reception (Freedburg 1989), the periods in which the buildings are viewed, thought about, and invested with other meanings by other social agents. Bonta has argued (1979) that there is a need for architectural history to be a history of meanings, and not just of forms (see Seidel 1999 for a demonstration of the point with respect to a Romanesque monument), and it is a view that I fully endorse.

Poststructuralism broadens the interpretative scope of structuralism almost immeasurably by its recognition of the contingencies and multiplicities of meaning, which is surely, *contra* Thomas Crow (1999), a positive development. It acknowledges that, even in the least likely contexts (such as patristic early Church history: Clark 2004) there are at least as many potential meanings as there are spectators, and that those spectators may change their interpretations depending on all sorts of circumstance. One can see from this the politics of poststructuralism: by denying that ownership of meaning is the preserve of those who build buildings, or of the social classes to which the patrons and their like belong, poststructuralism franchises audiences and democratises both architectural experience and the articulation of it. Poststructuralism redefines the receptors and respondents of architecture to be the architects of interpretation.

Historically, Romanesque scholars have not thought about language and meaning in this way. Their tendency towards structuralism has been accidental and unknowing, as I said above. Poststructuralism, like postmodernism, is a frontier further out, and Romanesque scholars have generally chosen *not* to explore it. Its relevance to Romanesque has never been established. I believe that poststructuralism's light embrace of relativism has rendered it culturally and politically offensive to the older scholars who have shaped Romanesque studies and who determine professional employment opportunities.

To close this section I will examine very briefly two recent comments on architecture and language, one of them specific to our period and the other a more general one.

First, Roger Stalley devotes a chapter of his *Early Medieval Architecture* to the issue of language, but in that chapter he simply runs through those elements of buildings that Charles Jencks would have described as 'words' (Jencks 1991: 39-62). There is no sense that Stalley understands the importance of communication and meaning to the concept of language. He views 'the language of architecture' – the actual title of the chapter – as a check-list of signs that signify nothing other than the geographical locations and chronologies of the buildings that bear them. Here is his closing statement on the issue:

> From time to time modern writers have questioned whether the notion of the 'Romanesque style' has any validity. So much variation exists between different regions in planning, structure, and sculptural embellishment, that it is easy to despair of finding any consistency. It is obvious, however, that architects in widely differing areas employed similar techniques to give *expression* to their buildings. Rather than insisting on Romanesque as a unified style, it is rather more useful to think of it in terms of a language, utilized by local masons according to their own traditions and aesthetic choices (Stalley 1999: 211; emphasis added).

To this statement I would simply add the comment that, having reviewed stylistic elements of the architecture under the heading of language, Stalley cannot query Romanesque's cohesion as a style and then, in the same breadth, suggest that it is a language or is language-like. If we follow his advice and think of it 'in terms of a language' we are *de facto* assuming it to have stylistic unity according to his own definition.

The second example is the editors' introduction to a collection of essays entitled *Architecture and Language.* Its authors, Georgia Clarke and Paul Crossley, are more sensitive than Stalley to the concept of language and to the theoretical issues surrounding the recourse of architectural historians to language, be it as model or metaphor. Yet, while their approach may be more sophisticated in its thinking, it is simply a more sophisticated structuralism. They share with the essayists in their book a belief in the primacy of the text, thereby privileging creators (both of the buildings-as-text and of the documents that refer to them) over audiences in a way that poststructuralists would reject:

> What unites all the contributions [to *Architecture and Language*] is their historical bias, their belief that any attempt to assimilate architecture to language must be judged on the specific historical relations between buildings and texts, and on the history of the architecture-language analogy itself. The theoretical links between the visual arts and language suggested by linguistic philosophy, structuralism, or the science of semiotics cannot and must not be ignored in any discussion of a unified theory of the arts, but nor can the theoretical issues be isolated from the particular pressures, values, conflicts, and interests that produced them. Critical analysis goes hand in hand with historical contextualisation (Clarke and Crossley 2000: 3).

5

Archaeology and Romanesque

So far in this book I have argued three interconnected points – or at least attempted to articulate three viewpoints – about Romanesque. The first is that the construct of the Romanesque style as defined on a pan-European scale is an inherently unstable one which has retained its cohesion by being 'black boxed'. The second, which uses the sociology of technology to do its theoretical heavy-lifting, is that the diverse architectures of eleventh- and twelfth-century Europe, hitherto treated as local or regional manifestations of some vaguely defined common ideal, can be read normatively as representing different stabilisations of the fragmented architectural inheritance from late Antiquity and the early middle ages. If Romanesque is to be a construct of value, I suggest, we must understand it to represent primarily the outcome of centrifugal forces originating in Antiquity rather than centripetal forces originating in the eleventh century. The third is that the buildings we are looking at were complex discursive objects of visual culture, located in, and contributing to, networks of understanding at a series of different levels. I want to finish now by returning to the question that provoked the writing of this book in the first instance.

Who understands Romanesque?

Two centuries after the pioneering work on the style by William Gunn and Charles de Gerville, Romanesque is now regarded by most scholars as fundamentally understood. While no specialist has said that in print before, at least to my knowledge, the assertion – not that Romanesque is understood but that it is regarded as understood – is sound.

The proof of this lies in part in the various published syntheses. They all tell the same story, albeit with differences of emphasis from one to another, and they all agree on the sites or objects – the St Savin-sur-Gartempe frescoes, the St Emmeram reliefs in Regensburg, the Gloucester candlestick, the Pisa campanile, and so on – that constitute the canon and which provide the framework in which lesser, non-canonical, sites and objects can be or should be interpreted. It is consensus scholarship, in terms of both investigative methodology and interpretative end-product. There is here what one might describe as *epistemological closure*. The nature and general content of knowledge in the sphere of Romanesque research have been established. It is significant that knowledge, experience and use of this art in the social world outside of and below the level of the eleventh- and twelfth-century intelligentsia who 'owned' these monuments and objects are not part of Romanesque's interpretative domain. Read again the quote from Clarke and Crossley above (p. 106), even though it is not specifically about Romanesque.

The proof of the assertion also lies in part in the more specialised literature on Romanesque's constituent media, where it is manifest in the identification and framing of problem issues. Studies of Romanesque iconography remain focused on scriptural exegesis and on the related matter of allegorical representations of political power; the consistency of methodology and language from one study to another is actually strikingly homologous with the art itself. In the literature on architecture, the engagement with iconography still has Richard Krautheimer's 1942 paper as its principal model, and therefore regards architectural iconography in exegetical terms. Much of the architectural literature, of course, is concerned with description of architectural detail, reconstruction of fragmentary buildings and building-parts, and argument for specific comparanda. But here too there is a strong sense of a framework of understanding that is sealed, or closed, epistemologically and ideologically. The methodology for dealing with the architectural record is established and is non-contentious. Disputes over problematic individual works occur within an established framework of understanding. Thus the alternative reconstructions of the east end of Tewkesbury (Fig. 9), to cite a well-known example of a problem monument in England, imply at most slightly different locations for the entire building in different places within the established model of 'English Romanesque' development, and assign to it different degrees of importance within that trajectory, but they do not arise from, nor do they translate into, different political or philosophical positions among the scholars engaged in the debate.

Fig. 9: The nave of Tewkesbury abbey church, looking north; there has been lively debate about the nature of its original east end.

As an archaeologist rather than an art historian, my judgement will doubtless be prejudiced, but, in attempting to understand this epistemological closure that I identify as characteristic of so much Romanesque architectural scholarship, I regard it as very significant that the interpretative study of the architecture has long been in the custody of the discipline of Art History, not Archaeology; it is a claim that I make simply on the basis of the institutional affiliations of so many of the scholars whose work is most accessible and whose views shape our perception of the material.

How and when the subject-matter relocated – or, rather, how and when the disciplines of Art History and Archaeology relocated themselves with respect to it – requires further study, but we should probably regard Art History's current custody of Romanesque architecture as an outcome of that same process of the 'art-ification' of architecture that Heinrich Wölfflin instituted for Art History in the late 1800s. Why it has remained within Art History when there is debate surrounding the natural disciplinary homes of 'architectural history' (see Jarzombek 1999) is another issue.

Whatever the historiography (and the future projection), it is certainly instructive to compare the modern literature generated by Art History's long-term engagement with Romanesque architecture with the modern literature generated by Archaeology's long-term engagement with the pan-European corpus of megalithic tomb architecture. The sheer diversity of approaches to and opinions on megalithic tombs, specifically with respect to their social contexts and meanings, reflects contemporary Archaeology's rejection of consensus scholarship, its acceptance of the principles of poststructuralism as a starting point in interpretation, and its constant exploration of new perspectives; it should be added that anybody who claims that archaeologists have the luxury of playing around with multiple approaches and interpretations because megalithic tombs are prehistoric objects is guilty of a fundamental misunderstanding of the nature of Archaeology as a discipline.

I do not intend to impugn the community of art historians by my observations. Art History has a long tradition of serious philosophical reflection on the complexities of meaning in art; Ernest Cassirer, for example, was as alert to the social contexts of art's meanings as any archaeologist over the past half century, while Erwin Panofsky addressed many of the concerns that archaeologists only turned to in the 1980s. Also, many art historians, especially since the days of the New Art History (Rees and Borzello 1986), would identify readily with contemporary Archaeology's concern with multivocality, its sensitivity to class and gender issues, and its acceptance of reflexive, even politically antagonistic, scholarship (see especially Forster 1972). However, practitioners within these more radical wings of the contemporary discipline of Art History have generally not been turning their gaze backwards in time to effect re-evaluations of medieval art, and have therefore left the field in more traditional hands. There is no reason to question the claim made more than ten years ago that the non-fixedness of meaning was 'one of the most fertile discoveries, indeed one of the themes of post-1970s art history' (Clayson 1995: 369), but such a discovery has not penetrated Romanesque architectural scholarship. And so I stand by my assertion that Romanesque architectural scholarship has had its epistemological shutters pulled down while in the custody of Art History.

Art History may, of course, have had this intellectual custody of Romanesque by default, since many archaeologists have shown little interest in Romanesque buildings beyond excavating their foundations, recording their details, and establishing their chronologies; indeed readers of the title of this book, *Archaeology and the Pan-European Romanesque*, may well have expected an up-to-date account of excavated findings. In an earlier publication I offered a more conspiratorial, and more obviously Marxian, thesis on the issue of Art History's guardianship of Romanesque (O'Keeffe 2003), and I will restate it here, even at the risk of offending (again) colleagues in a sister discipline. My thesis was that eleventh- and twelfth-century élites created and nourished the myth that its great church buildings were works of art rather than of craft, that they were objects of high culture to be understood in a particular way by few, not *de facto* objects of popular culture that could be understood in different ways by many. It was an undemocratic, anti-relativist, interpretation of art, and it was essential to their maintenance of social power. My thesis was also that the discipline of Art History, with its origins in the writings of Italian Renaissance and German Enlightenment intelligentsia (such as Vasari and Hegel, respectively), as well as with its traditional embrace of the concept of connoisseurship, has traditionally sought not to demystify and democratise that architecture but rather to maintain its identity, its hegemony even, as 'high art'. Readers of John Berger's work (1972) will recognise it as the seedbed of this idea. Archaeology, meanwhile, with its more humble origins, has acquiesced in the perpetuation of the 'high art' myth of Romanesque by not subjecting Romanesque works to its very particular methods of theoretical interrogation.

It should be clear from all this that my motivation in writing this book has been to argue for, and to expedite the passage to, a different type of scholarly engagement with these buildings, one that offers other ways of seeing. What most scholars understand Romanesque to be now, in 2007, is quite different from what Gunn and de Gerville understood it to be in the 1810s, or from what José Puig y Cadafalch and Arthur Kingsley Porter, for example, understood it to be when they started their research one hundred years later. Critically, it is not inconceivable that a century from now a claim can still be made that Romanesque is regarded as understood, but that it will be regarded as understood *then* in a different way from how it is regarded as understood *now*. We cannot claim to have reached now, in 2007, the final comprehension of the phenomenon. We cannot claim that the types of problem that we identify now will be the same types that scholars will fret over one hundred years from now, or that the interpretative frameworks in which problems like Tewkesbury's east end assume such importance will continue to endure.

To conclude...

What, to conclude, am I trying to say in this book? Let me clarify what I am *not* trying to say. This book is not an attack on that tradition of scholarship (in Art History, Architectural History or Archaeology) that regards as important the hunting down of textual sources for eleventh- and twelfth-century buildings, the lining up of these textual references with fabric, the determining of constructional sequences, and the rediscovery of the networks of knowledge by which buildings ended up looking as they do. On the contrary, these are important projects. They represent the 'craft' of traditional scholarship: one trains students to do these things. Rather, my argument is fundamentally that the normative interpretations of individual buildings and collectives of buildings that issue from this type of scrutiny say more about historiographic tradition than they do about architecture.

The principal target of my attack is on the mindset that conceives of the architecture as if this were not true. It is a fiction that these buildings are objects that can be represented truthfully by two dimensions, rather than places, environments, third-spaces even (see Soja 1996), that embody the very aspects of art that draw us towards them. It is a fiction that ultimately diminishes us. By robbing these buildings of their richness, it robs us – the modern spectators – of our capacity to self-discover through them and within them. We would do well to remember Meyer Schapiro's entanglement with medieval art works as described by Michael Holly – that he 'looked long and hard at past works not to authenticate, but to interrogate, and to be interrogated by' (1997: 9) – and to embrace such a challenge positively.

Bibliography

Addiss, James M., *Spatial Organisation in Romanesque Architecture* [1983] UMI (Ann Arbor, MI, 1987).

Armi, C.E., 'Orders and continuous orders in Romanesque architecture', *Journal of the Society of Architectural Historians* 34 (1975): 173-88.

——— *Masons and Sculptors in Romanesque Burgundy: The New Aesthetic of Cluny III* (University Park, PA, 1983).

——— 'The corbel table', *Gesta* 39 (2000): 89-116.

——— *Design and Construction in Romanesque Architecture. First Romanesque Architecture and the Pointed Arch in Burgundy and Northern Italy* (Cambridge, 2004).

Atroshenko, V.I. and Collins, Judith, *The Origins of the Romanesque: Near Eastern Influences on European Art, 4th-12th Centuries* (London, 1985).

Baltrušaitis, Jurgis, *La Stylistique Ornementale dans la Sculpture Romane* (Paris, 1931).

Barrett, J., 'Agency, the duality of structure, and the problem of the archaeological record', in Ian Hodder (ed.), *Archaeological Theory Today* (London, 2001): 141-64.

Barthes, Roland, *Elements of Semiology* (London, 1967).

Baudrillard, J., *Simulations, Semiotext(e)* (New York, 1983).

Benjamin, Walter, 'The work of art in the age of mechanical reproduction' [1936], in W. Benjamin, *Illuminations* (New York, 1969).

Benson, Robert L. and Constable, Giles (eds), *Renaissance and Renewal in the Twelfth Century* (Oxford, 1982).

Berger, John, *Ways of Seeing* (London, 1972).

Bijker, Wiebe, *Of Bicycles, Bakelites, and Bulbs: Toward a Theory of Sociotechnical Change* (Cambridge, MA, 1994).

——— and Law, John (eds), *Shaping Technology / Building Society Studies in Sociotechnological Change* (Cambridge, MA, 1992).

———, Hughes, T.P. and Pinch, T.J. (eds), *The Social Construction of Technological Systems* (Cambridge, MA, 1987).

Bizzarro, Tina Waldeier, *Romanesque Architectural Criticism: A Prehistory* (Cambridge, 1992).

Bloch, R. Howard and Nichols, Stephen G., 'Introduction', in Bloch and Nichols (eds), *Medievalism and the Modern Temper* (Baltimore, 1996): 1-24.

Bober, H., 'Editor's foreword', in E. Mâle, *Religious Art in France: The Twelfth Century. A Study of Religious Iconography* (Princeton, 1978): v-xxiv.

Boisseree, Sulpiz, *Geschichte und Beschreibung des Doms von Köln* (Stuttgart, 1823).

Bonde, S., Mark, R. and Robison, E.C., 'Walls and other vertical elements', in Robert Mark (ed.), *Architectural Technology up to the Scientific Revolution* (Cambridge, MA, 1993): 52-137.

Bonnell, V.E. and Hunt, L., 'Introduction', in Bonnell and Hunt (eds) *Beyond the Cultural Turn: New Directions in the Study of Society and Culture* (Berkeley, 1999): 1-34.

Bonta, Juan Pablo, *Architecture and its Interpretation: A Study of Expressive Systems in Architecture* (London, 1979).

Bony, J., 'Introduction', *Studies in Western Art I. Acts of the Twentieth International Congress of the History of Art* (Princeton, 1963): 81-4.

——— *French Gothic Architecture of the Twelfth and Thirteenth Centuries* (Berkeley, 1983).

Bresc-Bautier, G., 'Les imitations du St-Sépulchre de Jerusalem (IXe-XVe siècles). Archéologie d'une dévotion', *Revue d'Histoire de la Spiritualité* 50 (1974): 319-42.

Bynum, C.W., 'Did the twelfth century discover the individual?', *Journal of Ecclesiastical History* 1 (1980): 1-17.

Cabanot, Jean, *Les Débuts de la Sculpture Romane dans le Sud-Ouest du la France* (Paris, 1987).

Cahn, W., 'The artist as outlaw and apparatchik: freedom and constraint in the interpretation of medieval art', in Stephen Scher (ed.), *The Renaissance of the Twelfth Century* (Providence, 1969): 10-14.

——— 'Schapiro and Focillon', *Gesta* 41 (2002): 129-36.

Callon, Michel and Latour, Bruno, 'Unscrewing the big Leviathan: how actors macro-structure reality and how sociologists help them to do so', in K. Knorr-Cetina and A.V. Cicouvel (eds), *Advances in Social Theory and Methodology* (London, 1981): 277-303.

Camille, Michael, *Image on the Edge: The Margins of Medieval Art* (London, 1992).

——— 'How New York stole the idea of Romanesque art: medieval, modern and postmodern in Meyer Schapiro', *Oxford Art Journal* 17, 1 (1994): 65-75.

——— 'Prophets, canons, and promising monsters', *Art Bulletin* 78, 2 (1996): 198-201.

Carlsson, Frans, *The Iconology of Romanesque Tectonics* (Hassleholm, 1976).

Caskey, J., 'Whodunnit? Patronage, the canon, and the problematics of agency in Romanesque and Gothic art', in Conrad Rudolph (ed.), *A Companion to Medieval Art* (Oxford, 2006): 193-212.

Chaplin, S., 'Towards a history of medieval architecture', *Art History* 9, 3 (1986): 385-95.

Clark, Elizabeth A., *History, Theory, Text: Historians and the Linguistic Turn* (Cambridge, MA, 2004).

Clarke, Georgia and Crossley, Paul, *Architecture and Language: Constructing Identity in European Architecture, c. 1000 – c. 1650* (Cambridge, 2000).

Clayson, H., 'Materialist art history and its points of difficulty', *Art Bulletin* 77, 3 (1995): 367-71.

Cocke, T., 'Rediscovery of the Romanesque', in *English Romanesque Art 1066-1200* (London 1984): 360-6.

Conant, Kenneth John, *Carolingian and Romanesque Architecture 800-1200*, 1st edn (Harmondsworth, 1959).

——— *Cluny: Les Églises et la Maison du Chef d'Ordre* (Mâcon, 1968).

Constable, Giles, *The Reformation of the Twelfth Century* (Cambridge, 1996).

Corroyer, Edouard-Jules, *L'Architecture Romane* (Paris, 1888).

Crossley, P., 'Medieval architecture and meaning: the limits of iconography', *Burlington Magazine* 130 (1988): 116-21.

Crow, Thomas, *The Intelligence of Art* (Chapel Hill, NC, 1999).

Crozet, René, 'Problèmes de méthode: les théories françaises sur les écoles romanes', *Boletín del Semininario de Estudios de Arte y Arquelogíca* 21-2 (1954-6): 39-45.

Curran, Kathleen, *The Romanesque Revival: Religion, Politics and Transnational Exchange* (Pennsylvania, 2003).

De Caumont, A., 'Essai sur l'architecture religieuse de moyen âge', *Mémoires de la Société des Antiquaries de Normandie* 1 (1824): 537-677.

De Lasteyrie, R., *L'Architecture Religieuse en France à l'Epoque Romane* (Paris, 1911).

Dehio, George and Von Bezold, Gustav, *Die Kirchliche Baukunst des Abendlandes, Historisch und Systematisch Dargestellt*, 7 vols (Stuttgart, 1884-1901).

Deschamps, P., 'Notes sur la sculpture romane en Bourgogne', *Gazette des Beaux-Arts* 5th ser. 6 (1922): 61-80.

——— 'Etude sur la renaissance de la sculpture en France à l'époque romane', *Bulletin Monumental* 84 (1925): 5-98.

Deschoulières, F., 'La théorie d'Eugene Lefèvre-Pontalis sur les écoles romanes', *Bulletin Monumental* 84 (1925): 197-252; 85 (1926): 5-65.

Didron, Adolphe, *Iconographie Chrétienne* (Paris, 1845).

Dobres, M.A. and Robb, John (eds), *Agency in Archaeology* (London, 2000).

Durliat, M., 'La Catalogne et le première art roman', *Bulletin Monumental* 147 (1989): 209-38.
Dynes, W., 'Art, language and Romanesque ', *Gesta* 26 (1989): 3-10.
Eckstein, Hans, *Die romanische Architektur. Der Stil und seine Formen* (Köln, 1975).
Elkins, James, *Our Beautiful, Dry, and Distant Texts: Art History as Writing* (London, 2000).
Erlande-Brandenburg, A., *The Cathedral. The Social and Architectural Dynamics of Construction* (Cambridge, 1994).
Evans, Joan, *The Romanesque Architecture of the Order of Cluny* (Cambridge, 1938)
Feenberg, Andrew, *Questioning Technology* (London, 1999).
Fernie, Eric, *The Architecture of the Anglo-Saxons* (London, 1983).
——— 'Romanesque architecture', in Conrad Rudolph (ed.), *A Companion to Medieval Art* (Oxford, 2006): 295-313.
Fish, Stanley, *Is there a Text in this Class? The Authority of Interpretative Communities* (Cambridge, MA, 1980).
Fishman, J., 'Who speaks what language to whom and when?', *La Linguistique* 2 (1965): 67-88.
Focillon, Henri, *The Life of Forms in Art* (Paris, 1948).
——— *L'An Mil* (Paris, 1953).
Forster, K.W., 'Critical history of art, or transfiguration of values', *New Literary History* 3 (1972): 459-70.
Forty, Adrian, *Words and Buildings: A Vocabulary of Modern Architecture* (London, 2000).
Frankl, Paul, *Die frühmittelalterliche und romanische Baukunst* (Potsdam 1926).
——— *The Gothic: Literary Sources and Interpretations through Eight Centuries* (Princeton, 1960).
Freedburg, D., *The Power of Images: Studies in the History and Theory of Response* (Chicago, 1989).
Friedman, A.T., 'In this cold barn we dream', *Art Bulletin* 76, 4 (1994): 575-8.
Gardelles, J., 'Recherches sur les origines des façades à étages d'arcatures des églises médiévales', *Bulletin Monumental* 136 (1978): 113-33.
Gilchrist, Roberta, *Gender and Archaeology* (London, 1999).
Gimbutas, Marija, *The Language of the Goddess* (San Francisco, 1989).
Gloag, John, *The Architectural Interpretation of* History (London, 1975).
Gombrich, E. *Art and Illusion* (London, 1960).
Grodecki, Louis, *Au Seuil de l'Art Roman: l'Architecture Ottonienne* (Paris, 1958).
Gunn, William, *An Inquiry into the Origin and Influence of Gothic Architecture* (London, 1819).

Habermas, J., *The Theory of Communicative Action* (London, 1981).
Haskins, C.H., *The Renaissance of the Twelfth Century* (Cambridge, MA, 1927).
Hazan, O., *Le Mythe du Progrès Artistique* (Montreal, 1999).
Hearn, M.F., *Romanesque Sculpture: The Revival of Monumental Stone Sculpture in the Eleventh and Twelfth Centuries* (London, 1981).
Heitz, Carol, *L'Architecture Religieuse Carolingienne: Les Formes et leurs Fonctions* (Paris, 1980).
Heslop, T.A. 'Late Twelfth-century writing about art, and aesthetic relativity,' in Gale R. Owen-Crocker and Timothy Graham (eds), *Medieval Art: Recent Perspectives* (Manchester, 1998): 129-41.
Hills, P., 'Meyer Schapiro, Art Front, and the Popular Front', *Oxford Art Journal* 17 (1994): 30-41.
Holly, Michael A., *Panofsky and the Foundations of Art History* (Ithaca, 1984).
——— 'Schapiro style', *Journal of Aesthetics and Art Criticism* 55, 1 (1997): 6-10.
Jarzombek, M., 'The disciplinary dislocations of (architectural) history', *Journal of the Society of Architectural Historians* 58, 3 (1999): 488-93.
Jencks, Charles, *The Language of Post-Modern Architecture* (London, 1991).
Jones, Owen, *The Grammar of Ornament* (London, 1856).
Kendall, C.B., *The Allegory of the Church: Romanesque Portals and their Verse Inscriptions* (Toronto, 1998).
Kidson, P. 'Panofsky, Suger and Saint-Denis', *Journal of the Warburg and Courtauld Institutes* 50 (1987): 1-17.
Krautheimer, R., 'Introduction to an "iconography of medieval architecture"', *Journal of the Warburg and Courtauld Institutes* 5 (1942): 1-33.
Kubach, Hans Erich, *Romanesque Architecture* (New York, 1975).
Kuhn, Thomas, *The Structure of Scientific Revolutions* [1962] (Chicago, 1996).
Landes, R., 'The fear of the apocalyptic year 1000: Augustinian historiography, medieval and modern', *Speculum* 75 (2000): 97-145.
Lasko, P., *Ars Sacra 800-1200* (Harmondsworth, 1972).
Law, John, *A Sociology of Monsters: Essays on Power, Technology and Domination* (London, 1991).
Lyman, T.W., 'L'intégration du portail dans la façade méridionale', *Cahiers de St Michel de Cuxa* 8 (1977): 55-68.
Mainstone, R.J., 'Structural analysis, structural insights, and historical interpretation', *Journal of the Society of Architectural Historians* 56, 3 (1997): 316-40.

Mâle, Emile, *L'Art Allemand et l'Art Française au Moyen-Age* (Paris, 1917).

——— *L'Art Religieux au XIIe Siècle en France* (1922); English translation: *Religious Art in France: The Twelfth Century. A Study of Religious Iconography* (Princeton, 1978).

Malone, C.M., 'St. Bénigne in Dijon as exemplum of Rodulf Glaber's metaphoric "White Mantle"', in Nigel Hiscock (ed.), *The White Mantle of Churches: Architecture, Liturgy and Art around the Millennium* (Turnhout, 2003): 160-79.

Martin, J., 'Classicism and style in Latin literature', in Benson and Constable (eds), *Renaissance and Renewal in the Twelfth Century* (Oxford, 1982): 537-68.

McClendon, Charles B., *The Origins of Medieval Architecture. Building in Europe AD 600-900* (New Haven, 2005).

McCormick, Michael, *Origins of the European Economy: Communications and Commerce, AD 300-900* (Cambridge, 2002).

McKitterick, R. (ed.), *Carolingian Culture: Emulation and Innovation* (Cambridge, 1994).

McNamara, J.A., 'The Herrenfrage: the restructuring of the gender system, 1050-1150', in Clare A. Lees (ed.), *Medieval Masculinities: Regarding Men in the Middle Ages* (Minneapolis, 1994): 3-29.

Melve, L., ' "The revolt of the medievalists". Direction in recent research on the twelfth-century renaissance', *Journal of Medieval History* 32 (2006): 231-52.

Mitcham, C. (ed.), *Social and Philosophical Constructions of Technology* (Greenwich, Conn., 1995).

Morrison, Karl, *History as a Visual Art in the Twelfth-Century Renaissance* (Princeton, 1990).

Nichols, Stephen G., *Romanesque Signs: Early Medieval Narrative and Iconography* (New Haven, 1983).

O'Keeffe, T., 'Architectural traditions of the early medieval church in Munster', in M.A. Monk and J. Sheehan (eds), *Early Medieval Munster* (Cork, 1998): 112-24.

——— *Romanesque Ireland: Architecture and Ideology in the Twelfth Century* (Dublin, 2003).

——— *Ireland's Round Towers: Buildings, Rituals and Landscapes of the Early Irish Church* (Stroud, 2004).

——— 'Landscape and memory: historiography, theory, methodology', in Y. Whelan and N. Moore (eds), *Heritage, Memory and the Politics of Space: New Perspectives on the Cultural Landscape* (Aldershot, 2006a).

——— 'Wheels of words, networks of knowledge: Romanesque scholarship and Cormac's Chapel', in D. Bracken and D. Ó Riain-Raedel (eds), *Ireland and Europe in the Twelfth Century: Reform and Renewal* (Dublin, 2006b): 257-69.

Oursel, Raymond, *Floraison de la Sculpture Romane*. 2 vols (La-Pierre-qui-Vire, 1973, 1976).
——— *Invention de l'Architecture Romane* (La-Pierre-qui-Vire, 1986).
Panofsky, Erwin, *Meaning in the Visual Arts* (London, 1955).
——— *Renaissance and Renascences in Western Art* (Stockholm, 1960).
Payne, A., 'Architectural history and the history of art: a suspended dialogue', *Journal of the Society of Architectural Historians* 58, 3 (1999): 292-9.
Pevsner, Nikolaus, *The Englishness of English Art* (London, 1956).
Plant, R., 'Architectural developments in the empire north of the Alps: the patronage of the imperial court', in Nigel Hiscock (ed.), *The White Mantle of Churches: Architecture, Liturgy and Art around the Millennium* (Turnhout, 2003): 29-56.
Pollock, G., 'The case of the missing women', in Mieke Bal and Inge Boer (eds), *The Point of Theory: Practices of Cultural Analysis* (New York, 1994): 91-108.
Porter, Arthur Kingsley, 'The rise of Romanesque sculpture', *American Journal of Archaeology* 22 (1918): 399-427.
——— 'La sculpture du XIIe siècle en Bourgogne', *Gazette des Beaux-Arts* 5th ser. 2 (1920): 73-94.
Powell, R.J., 'Art, history, and vision', *Art Bulletin* 77, 3 (1995): 379-82.
Potts, Alex, *Flesh and the Ideal: Winckelmann and the Origins of Art History* (New Haven, 2000).
Priego, Carlos Cid, *Arte Prerománico de la Monarquía Asturiana* (Oviedo, 1995).
Puig y Cadafalch, J., 'Decorative forms of the First Romanesque style', *Art Studies* 4 (1926): 11-99.
——— *Le Premier Art Romane: l'Architecture en Catalogne et dans l'Occident Méditerranéen aux Dixième et Onzième Siècles* (Paris, 1928).
——— *La Geographie et les Origines du Premier Art Roman* (Paris, 1935).
Pugin, A.W.N., *The True Principles of Pointed or Christian Architecture* (London, 1841).
Quicherat, J., 'De l'architecture romane', *Revue Archéologique* 8 (1851): 145-58.
Rebourg, A., *Autun*, 2 vols (Paris, 1993).
Rees, A.L. and Borzello, F. (eds), *The New Art History* (London, 1986).
Reuter, T., *Germany in the Early Middle Ages, c. 800-1056* (London, 1991).
Riegl, Alois, *Stilfragen: Grundlegungen zu einer Geschichte der Ornamentik* (Berlin, 1893).
Roosval, J., *Bonniers Konsthistoria* (Stockholm, 1930).
Rudolph, Conrad, *The 'Things of Greater Importance': Bernard of*

Clairvaux's Apologia and the Medieval Attitude toward Art (Philadelphia, 1990).
——— (ed.), *A Companion to Medieval Art* (Oxford, 2006).
Ruprich-Robert, V., *L'Architecture Normande aux XIe et XIIe Siècles en Normandie et en Angleterre*, 2 vols (Paris, 1887).
Salvini, R., 'Pre-Romanesque Ottonian and Romanesque ', *Journal of the British Archaeological Association* 3rd ser. 30 (1970): 1-20.
Sauerländer, W., 'Style or transition? The fallacies of classification discussed in the light of German architecture 1190-1260', *Architectural History* 30 (1987): 1-29.
Schapiro, M., 'The sculpture of Souillac [1931]', in *Selected Papers: Romanesque Art* (New York, 1977): 102-30.
——— 'On geometrical schematism in Romanesque art [1933]', in *Selected Papers: Romanesque Art* (New York, 1977): 265-84.
——— 'The New Viennese School', *Art Bulletin* 18 (1936): 258-66.
——— 'From Mozarabic to Romanesque in Silos [1939]', in *Selected Papers: Romanesque Art* (New York, 1977): 28-101.
——— 'On the aesthetic attitude in Romanesque art [1947]', in *Selected Papers: Romanesque Art* (New York, 1977): 1-27.
——— 'Style [1962]', in *Selected Papers: Theory and Philosophy of Art: Style, Artist, and Society* (New York, 1994): 51-101.
Seidel, Linda, *Songs of Glory. The Romanesque Façades of Aquitaine* (Chicago, 1981).
——— *Legends in Limestone: Lazarus, Gislebertus, and the Cathedral of Autun* (Chicago, 1999).
Shanks, M. and Tilley, C., *Reconstructing Archaeology. Theory and Practice*, 2nd edn (London, 1992).
Snyder, J., 'Nineteenth-century photography of sculpture and the rhetoric of substitution', in G. Johnson (ed.), *Sculpture and Photography: Envisioning the Third Dimension* (Cambridge, 1998): 21-34.
Soja, Edward, W., *Thirdspace: Expanding the Geographical Imagination* (Oxford, 1996).
Soufflet, P., 'Continental influences on English Romanesque sculpture', *Oxford Art Journal* 4, 2 (1981): 5-9.
Stalley, Roger, *Early Medieval Architecture* (Oxford, 1999).
Strzygowski, Josef, *Orient oder Rom* (Leipzig, 1910).
——— *Ursprung der Christlichen Kirchenkunst* (Leipzig, 1920).
Summerson, J. *The Classical Language of Architecture* (London, 1963).
Swanson, R.N., *The Twelfth-Century Renaissance* (Manchester, 1999).
Taylor, K.F., 'Architecture's place in art history: art or adjunct', *Art Bulletin* 83, 2 (2001): 342-6.
Vergnolle, E., 'Chronologie et méthode d'analyse: doctrines sur les débuts de la sculpture romane en France', *Cahiers de St Michel de Cuxa* 9 (1978): 141-62.
——— *L'Art Roman en France* (Paris, 1994).

Vesely, Dalibor, *Architecture in the Age of Divided Representation. The Question of Creativity in the Shadow of Production* (Cambridge, Mass., 2004).
Vidler, A., 'Technologies of space/spaces of technology', *Journal of the Society of Architectural Historians* 58, 3 (1999): 482-86.
Viollet-le-Duc, Eugène-Emmanuel, *Dictionnaire Raisonné de l'Architecture Française du Onzième Siècle au Seizième Siècle,* 10 vols (Paris, 1854-68).
Von Winterfeld, D., *Der Dom in Bamberg*, 2 vols (Berlin, 1979).
White, H., 'Afterword', in V.E. Bonnell and L. Hunt (eds), *Beyond the Cultural Turn: New Directions in the Study of Society and Culture* (Berkeley, 1999): 315-24.
Williams, John, 'Meyer Schapiro in Silos: pursuing an iconography of style', *Art Bulletin* 85, 3 (2003): 442-68.
Wirth, Jean, *L'Image Médiévale: Naissance et Développements (Vie-XV Siècles)* (Paris, 1989).
——— *L'Image à l'Époque Romane* (Paris, 1999).
Wright, Roger, *Late Latin and Early Romance in Spain and Carolingian France* (Liverpool, 1982).
Wyss, Beat, *Hegel's Art History and the Critique of Modernity* (Cambridge, 1999).
Zarnecki, George, *Romanesque* (London, 1989).

Index

Aachen, 37
Abbot Suger of St Denis, 43, 83, 89
actor-network theory (ANT), 90-1, 93, 94
Addiss, James, 81, 83
aesthetic taste, interpretation, 14, 33, 36, 67, 78, 82, 105
agency, 42-3, 64, 70, 71, 89
Alcuin, 31
Anglo-Norman architecture, 54
Antiquity, 9, 98, 107
Archaeology, 110-12, 113
architectural decoration, 84
architectural history, 103, 110, 113
architectural iconography, 37, 108
Aristotle, 82
Armi, E. Edson, 49
'art' versus 'craft', 70
Art Bulletin, 42
Art History, 8, 9, 11, 42, 47, 66, 69, 71, 72, 79, 80, 110-12, 113
articulation, 53, 101
ashlar, 62-3
Asturia, 52
Autun, 19, 21

Baltrušaitis, Jurgis, 39-40, 84
Bamberg, 21
Baudrillard, Jean, 76
bay-division, 16, 19, 49
Beaune, 19
Benedictines, 17, 18-19
Berger, John, 112
Bernard of Clairvaux, 83
Bijket, Weibe, 93
'Black Box', 10, 65-6, 71, 73, 91, 97, 107
Bloch, Howard, 56, 57
Blondel, Charles, 58
bodily space, 80
Bonta, Juan Pablo, 103
Bony, Jean, 48
Book of Revelation, 14
Brixworth, 46
Burgundy, 17, 50
Bynum, Caroline, 43
Byzantine empire, 52, 67

Camille, Michael, 41
canon, the idea of, 75, 77
capitals, 19, 20, 38, 56, 85
Carlsson, Frans, 40
Carolingian renaissance, 21, 23, 25, 35, 36, 47, 48, 49, 68, 98
Cartesian interpretations, 82
Cassirer, Ernest, 111
Catalonia, 48, 49, 50
Charlemagne, 37
chronology, 14, 49, 50, 51
Civray, St Nicolas, 21
Clarke, Georgia, 105
class, 48-9
classicism, 99
Cluny, 16-19, 20, 23, 29, 37, 38, 56, 74

Collon, Michel, 91
Conant, Kenneth, 10, 19, 36, 37, 48, 54, 61, 64, 74, 76, 77, 78
Constantinian architecture, 23
Constantinople, 52
corbel tables, 8, 49
corporeal identity, 80
Council of Tours (813), 31
Crossley, Paul, 105,
Crow, Thomas, 104
Crozet, René, 48
culturalism, 63, 64, 73, 83, 88, 92

De Caumont, Arcisse, 30
De Gerville, Charles, 30, 31, 54, 69, 98, 107, 112
De Lasteyrie, Robert, 34, 61
Dehio and von Bezold, 76
Deschamps, Paul, 34-5, 38
dialectic, 69, 70
Didron, Adolphe, 29, 34
Doric order, 57
Durham Castle, 53
Durham Cathedral, 23, 46, 80-1
Dynes, Wayne, 32

early Church history, 104
Elkins, James, 77
Ely Cathedral, 17
engineering, 54, 86-7
England, 29, 30, 32, 109
English Romanesque, 109
Enlightenment, 112
epistemology, 55, 72, 108. 110, 111
ethnicity, 56
Europe, 7, 10, 13, 14, 15, 17, 18, 20, 21, 23, 25, 52, 66-8, 75, 76, 93, 96, 107; Mediterranean Europe, 28, 47, 48; Northern Europe, 28-9, 47, 48, 49, 50, 60, 72; Southern Europe, 47, 49, 50; Western Europe, 50
Evans, Joan, 57
ex oriente lux, 47

façades, 62
Félebien, André, 29
Fernie, Eric, 50, 52, 54, 63, 66
feudalism, 54
'First Romanesque', 48, 49, 52
flying buttresses, 19
Focillon, Henri, 38-9, 40, 41, 48, 53, 78, 85
formalism, 39-41, 42
France, 29-30, 32, 33-4, 49, 60, 76, 83, 84
Frankl, Paul, 35-6, 48, 70
Fulda, 21

Gaul, 15, 21
gender, 57, 58-9
Germany, 30, 32, 60, 60
Glaber, Rodulfus, 15
Gloucester candlestick, 108
Gombrich, Ernst, 24, 97
Gothic, 14, 25, 26, 28, 29-30, 32-3, 34, 35, 42, 43, 51, 54, 70, 85-6, 88, 89
Goths, 28
Grodecki, Louis, 48
Gunn, William, 30, 54, 69, 107, 112

Habermas, Jürgen, 89
Hazan, Olga, 54
Hearn, M.F., 40
Hedingham Castle, Fig. 7
Hegel, G.W.F., 69, 70
Hegelianism, 40, 70, 71, 97
Henry, Françoise, 39
Hiberno-Saxon world, 52
Hildebert of Lavardin, 99
historiography, 20-44, 46, 57, 85, 97, 102, 110
Holly, Michael, 114
Holy Sepulchre, Jerusalem, 37
Horn, Walter, 48

Hugo, Victor, 29

ideology, 89
illuminated books, 26
Information Technology, 63-4, 74
Ionic order, 57
Ireland, 23
Italy, 15, 28, 60

Jencks, Charles, 104

Krautheimer, Richard, 37, 108
Kubach, Hans Erich, 10, 36, 48, 54, 64, 76, 77, 78, 90
Kuhn, Thomas, 88, 92
Kunstwollen, 69, 70, 72

l'an mil, 16, 36
La-Charité-sur-Loire, 19
language, 23, 31-2, 54, 98-100
Laon, 46
Lasko, Peter, 46
Latin, 98-100
Latour, Bruno, 91
linguistics, 64, 72, 99, 100-6
Loire valley, 50
Lombardy, 49, 50
luminosity, 81

Mainz, 23
Mâle, Emile, 34, 38, 43, 85
Marxism, 37, 41, 49, 69, 70, 112
massing, 17, 19, 53, 85
Maxwell, Robert, 42
mechanical reproduction, 75, 76, 77, 78
megalithic tombs, 110-11
metalwork, 26
metaphor, 57, 65, 66, 101, 105
Milan, 20
millennialism, 15
modernity, 67
monasticism, 17, 36, 54
Mont-St-Michel, 23
Moreland, John, 8
Morrison, Karl, 58
Musée des Monuments Française, 75

Naranco, 50
new medievalism, 56
Nichols, Stephen, 37, 52, 56, 57
Norman architecture, 54
Notre-Dame-le-Grande, Poitiers, Fig. 5

Ottonian renaissance, 21, 35, 36, 48
Oursel, Raymond, 27

Panofsky, Erwin, 20, 32, 43, 111
Paray-le-Monial, 19
Paris Basin, 14, 25
patronage, 43, 46-7, 54
perspective, 80
Peterborough cathedral, 17
Pevsner, Nikolas, 47
phenomenology, 45, 75, 81-2
philology, 56, 57
photography, 75, 76, 77, 78-9, 80
piers, 49
pilasters, 49, 62, 80
pilgrimage, 36, 54
Pisa, 23
Plato, 69
Platonic philosophy, 27, 69
Po valley, 48
poesis, 82
politics of academia, 66, 104
Porter, Arthur Kingsley, 35, 38, 41, 112
positivism, 73, 92
poststructuralism, 100-6, 110
'pre-Romanesque', 35, 36, 50, 84
Protestantism, 34, 69
'proto-Romanesque', 35, 36, 50
psychoanalysis, 80
Puig y Cadafalch, Josef, 32, 48, 49, 112

Quicherat, Jules, 31-2

race, 47
Ramiro I of Asturia, 50
Ravenna, 20
reform movements, 15, 36
regionalism, regional schools, 33, 37, 46-51, 62, 68, 75, 83-4, 89-96, 105, 107
relativism, 73
Renaissance, twelfth-century, 14, 22, 68, 71
Renaissance, Italian, 24, 28, 56, 80, 112
Rhineland, 50
Riegl, Alois, 69
Roman architecture, 13, 20, 21, 23, 24, 25, 32, 36, 47, 48, 62, 65, 95
Roman empire, 28
romanitas, 20, 21, 22, 65, 68, 91, 96, 99
Rome, 20, 99
Roosval, Jonny, 48
Ruprich-Robert, V., 33

Salvini, Roberto, 32, 48-9
San Miniato, 20
St Benedict, Rule of, 17
St Denis, 14, 25, 43, 89
St Emmeran, Regensburg, 108
St Etienne, Caen, 53
St Giles-du-Gard, 72, 99
St Peter's, Rome, 20, 21, 37
St Philibert, Tournus, 19
St Savin-sur-Gartempe, 108
St Sernin, Toulouse, 23
St Vincent, Cardona, 53
Ste Madeleine, Vézeley, 23
Sant'Ambrogio, Milan, 23
Santiago de Compostella, 23, 46
Saussurean linguistic theory, 100
Saxony, 50
Schapiro, Meyer, 38, 40-1, 66, 70, 84, 97, 114
scientism, 63, 64, 73, 82, 83, 88
sculpture, 37, 38-41, 42, 49, 75, 77, 84-5, 102, 105
Second Vatican Council, 24, 66
Seidel, Linda, 42
semiotics, 106
sex, 56, 57-60
Shanks, Michael, 8
simulacrum/simulacra, 76, 77
Silos, 41
smell, 81
social construction of technology (SCOT), 65, 90-1, 93, 94, 107
social constructivism, 87, 90-1, 93, 95
Soufflet, Pascal, 27
Speyer, 23
spolia, 21
stave churches, 72
Stalley, Roger, 54-5, 76, 77, 78, 104-5
structuralism, 100-6
Strzygowski, Josef, 47
style, 45, 55, 64, 66, 67, 69-72, 73, 97-8
symbolic interpretations, 82
symbolism, 54

techne, 82
technology, 70, 75, 84, 85-96
telos, teleology, 69, 91
temperature, 81
Tewkesbury, 109, 113, Fig. 9
text, 105
texture, 81
theosis, 37
Tilley, Christopher, 8
towers, 16, 19, 85, 86, 89

Urnes, 72

Vasari, Georgio, 28

vaults, 16, 19, 49, 62-3, 85, 86, 87, 89
Vergnolle, Elaine, 36
Vesely, Dalibor, 82
vie des formes, 53, 54
Viollet-le-Duc, Eugène-Emmanuel, 32, 33, 76
Visigothic Spain, 52
Vitruvius, 57
Von Simson, Otto, 43

wall paintings, 26
Winkelmann, J.J., 58, 69
Wölfflin, Heinrich, 79, 110
women, 57

Zarnecki, George, 51, 52, 54, 55, 66, 93
Zeitgeist, 50-1, 52, 69, 97
Zodiaque books, 37, 78, 83